MASTERY LEARNING IN CLASSROOM INSTRUCTION

A Title in the CURRENT TOPICS IN CLASSROOM INSTRUCTION Series

James H. Block
*University of California
Santa Barbara*

Lorin W. Anderson
University of South Carolina

Macmillan Publishing Co., Inc.
New York
Collier Macmillan Publishers
London

TO
LYNNE AND DIANNE

Macmillan Publishing Co., Inc.
866 Third Avenue, New York, New York 10022

Collier-Macmillan Canada, Ltd.

Library of Congress Cataloging in Publication Data

Block, James H
  Mastery learning in classroom instruction.

  (Current topics in classroom instruction series)
  Includes bibliographies and index.
  1. Teaching. 2. Lesson planning. I. Anderson,
Lorin W., joint author. II. Title.
LB1025.2.B59   371.1'02   75-2043
ISBN 0-02-311000-7

Printing: 1 2 3 4 5 6 7 8   Year: 5 6 7 8 9 0

Preface

Mastery learning is a teaching philosophy asserting that under appropriate instructional conditions virtually *all* students can learn well most of what they are taught in school. The purpose of this small volume is to lay out one practical strategy whereby this philosophy can be implemented in the classroom.

The strategy we shall describe is designed for use primarily by an *in-service* elementary or secondary school teacher. It assumes that the in-service teacher faces pressure to cover a basically fixed curriculum in a fixed period of calendar time; that the bulk of this curriculum is contained in one or more prescribed textbooks; that the teacher already possesses some group-based techniques for teaching each textbook's material to a class; and that the teacher's students possess different individual learning requirements. *In short, our mastery learning strategy is designed to supplement and to better individualize the in-service teacher's customary group-based techniques so that the teacher can teach textbook materials for mastery within the instructional time available.*

Let us make clear from the outset that our strategy is not a painless cure for all of the instructional problems facing the in-service teacher. Teaching for mastery takes time and effort. But our approach has yielded dramatically and consistently improved student learning under a wide variety of instructional conditions both here and abroad. You, the reader, will have to decide whether the chance to have a consistently positive impact on the learning of most of your students, rather than a few, is worth the time and effort that teaching of mastery will require.

Acknowledgments

Any book is ultimately people—people writing, researching, typing, editing, and revising. This book was fortunate to have the following individuals help in its production:

iii

57042

Dr. Benjamin S. Bloom—Ben turned us on to the idea of mastery learning and has been a constant source of ideas and advice as we have sought to implement mastery learning ideas in the classroom.

Dr. Norman E. Gronlund—Dr. Gronlund was kind enough to solicit this volume for inclusion in Macmillan's *Current Topics in Classroom Instruction* series.

Dr. Joseph P. Ryan—Joe provided us with constructive criticism as well as suggestions for questions to appear in the final chapter.

Bonnie Balfour, *Cooky Chaplin*, and *Elaine Grove*—Bonnie typed the initial drafts of the manuscript; Cooky typed the intermediate draft; and Elaine typed the final draft—over the hectic Christmas holiday season, we might add.

Corinne Scott, Vana Meredith, and *Lynne Cantlay*—Corinne and Vana provided valuable research and editing assistance as we assembled the initial and intermediate drafts of the manuscript. Lynne was instrumental in the production of the final product. She helped edit, revise, and retype page after page.

Our special thanks to all of you!

Santa Barbara, California   J. H. B.

Columbia, South Carolina   L. W. A.

Contents

Chapter 1

Mastery Learning: An Overview

Mastery learning is a philosophy about teaching. It asserts that under appropriate instructional conditions virtually all students can and will learn well most of what they are taught.

The roots of this philosophy go back several hundred years. But only in roughly the last decade have teaching strategies been developed whereby it might be feasibly implemented in the classroom. The purpose of this small volume is to develop one of these strategies.

The mastery learning strategy we will propose will be a *group-based* approach to individualized instruction in which students can learn *cooperatively* with their classmates. The approach will attempt to better individualize instruction by clearly defining what the students will be expected to learn and to what level, by giving them additional time to learn, and by helping them when and where they have learning difficulties. The reader is referred to Block (1971, 1973a, 1974) for descriptions of more *individually based* mastery approaches in which students can learn *independently* of their peers.

Let us be clear from the outset. The approach we are about to describe is not a panacea for all the instructional problems facing the classroom teacher. It is, however, an approach to classroom instruction that has consistently yielded improved student learning under a wide variety of classroom conditions (Block, 1971, 1974; Peterson, 1972).

The Bloom-Block "Learning for Mastery" Strategy

The genesis for our mastery learning ideas was a conceptual model of school learning suggested by John B. Carroll (1963). This model derived from the observation that a student's aptitude for a particular subject predicted either the level to which he could learn the subject in a given time or the time he would require to learn it to a given level.

Hence, rather than defining aptitude as an index of the level to which a student could learn, Carroll defined aptitude as a measure of *learning rate*, i.e., as a measure of the amount of time the student would require to learn a given level under ideal instructional conditions. A student with high aptitude for a subject would learn it quickly, while one with a low aptitude would learn it more slowly.

In its simplest form, Carroll's model proposed that if each student was allowed the time he needed to learn to some criterion level and if he spent the necessary time, then he would probably attain the level. However, if the pupil was not allowed enough time or did not spend the required time, then the degree to which he would learn could be expressed as follows:

$$\text{Degree of School Learning} = f\left(\frac{\text{time spent}}{\text{time needed}}\right)$$

In words, the *degree of school learning will depend on the time the student actually spent in learning relative to the time he needed to spend.*

Carroll believed that in the school situation the time spent and the time needed were influenced not only by learner characteristics but also by the characteristics of the instruction. The time spent was determined by either the student's *perseverance* (the amount of time he is willing to spend actively engaged in learning) or his *opportunity to learn* (the classroom time allotted to learning). If his opportunity to learn was greater than his perseverance, then his perseverance determined the time spent in learning. If his perseverance was greater than his opportunity to learn, then the reverse was true.

The time needed, on the other hand, was determined by the student's *aptitude* for the subject, the *quality of instruction* (including the instructional materials) and his *ability to understand this instruction*. If the quality of instruction was high, then the student would readily understand it and would need little time to learn the subject beyond that required by his aptitude. But if the quality of instruction was low, then the student would need more time.

The complete Carroll model proposed therefore:

$$\text{Degree of School Learning} = f\left(\begin{array}{l} \text{1. Perseverance}\quad \text{2. Opportunity to learn} \\ \text{3. Aptitude}\quad \text{4. Quality of Instruction} \\ \text{5. Ability to Understand Instruction} \end{array}\right)$$

In words, the *degree of school learning of a given subject depends on the student's perseverance or his opportunity to learn, relative to his aptitude for the subject, the quality of his instruction, and his ability to understand this instruction.*

Benjamin S. Bloom (1968) transformed this conceptual model into a working model for mastery learning by the following logic. If aptitude was predictive of the rate, but not necessarily the level, to which a student could learn, it should have been possible to fix the degree of school learning expected of each student at some mastery performance level. Then, by attending to the opportunity to learn and the quality of instruction—the variables under teacher control in Carroll's model—the teacher should have been able to ensure that each student attained this level.

Elaborating on this logic, Bloom argued that if students were normally distributed with respect to aptitude for some subject and were provided with *uniform* opportunity to learn and *uniform* quality of instruction, then few students will attain mastery. But if each student received *differential* opportunity to learn and *differential* quality of instruction, then a majority of students, perhaps as many as 95%, could be expected to attain mastery. We can represent Bloom's logic as follows:

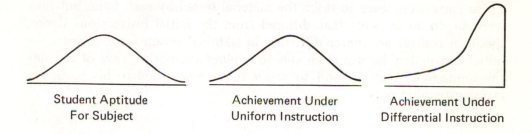

| Student Aptitude For Subject | Achievement Under Uniform Instruction | Achievement Under Differential Instruction |

In accordance with this logic, Bloom next sketched the outline for a mastery learning strategy that might be used in the typical classroom situation. Block (1971, 1973b) then refined and elaborated upon this outline so as to translate Bloom's ideas into a workable classroom strategy.

As noted above, Carroll's (1963) model of school learning proposed that each student could master a given subject if he was provided the time he needed to learn. Block's strategy attempted to minimize the time a student needed to learn so that it was within the fixed amount of calendar time available for instruction. This was accomplished through two distinct sets of steps, designed to maximize the quality of the classroom instruction. One set, the preconditions, occurred prior to the actual classroom instruction. The second, the operating procedures, took place in the classroom itself.

Preconditions for Mastery Learning

In Block's strategy, the teacher began by adopting the view that most of his students *could* learn well and that he could teach so that most *would* learn well. The teacher then turned to the problem of formulating what he meant by mastery of his subject. Here, the teacher first defined what all students would be expected to learn. This entailed the formulation of a set of course instructional objectives. He then determined to what level or mastery performance standard all students would be expected to achieve these objectives. Finally, the teacher prepared a final examination over all these objectives for administration at the close of his instruction. Each student's score on this test was to be compared against a preset mastery level of test performance.

Next, the teacher broke his course into a sequence of smaller teaching-learning units, where each unit typically covered about two weeks' worth of objectives. Then he developed simple feedback/correction procedures for each unit. First, he constructed a brief, ungraded diagnostic-progress test. This test was to provide specific information or feedback to both the teacher and the student about how the latter's learning was changing as a result of the initial instruction for the unit. Next, he developed a set of alternative instructional materials or "correctives" keyed to each item on the unit test. These correctives were to teach the material tested by each item, but they were to do so in ways that differed from the initial instruction. Hence, should a student encounter difficulty in learning certain material from the initial instruction, he would be able to explore alternative ways of learning the unmastered material and to select those best suited to his particular learning requirements.

Operating Procedures

The teacher was now ready to teach. Since students were not accustomed to learning for mastery or the notion that they all might earn A's, Block proposed that the teacher should spend some time at the outset orienting his students to the procedures to be used. He believed that this orientation period, combined with continual encouragement, support, and positive evidence of learning success, should develop in most students the belief that they could learn and hence the motivation to learn.

Following this period, Block suggested that the teacher teach the first unit using his customary group-based instructional methods. When this initial instruction was completed, and before moving on to the next unit, the teacher was to administer the unit diagnostic-progress test. Using the results of this test the teacher was to certify the progress of those students who were achieving as desired and to encourage those who were not progressing satisfactorily to use the unit's correctives to complete their learning. These latter students were then given the responsibility of completing their learning of the present unit before the initial instruction for the next unit began.

This cycle of group-based initial instruction, diagnostic-progress testing, and certification or individual correction was then repeated on each learning unit until all units had been completed. Lastly, the final examination was administered. All students who scored above the preset mastery performance level on this test earned "A"s or their equivalent.

Mastery Learning in the Classroom: Some Student Learning Outcomes

In the years since the publication of Bloom's 1968 paper "Learning for Mastery" and Block's 1971 book *Mastery Learning: Theory and Practice*, much school-based mastery learning research has been carried out around the world, at all levels of education. This research has occurred in all types of schools, in an increasingly wide variety of basic and more specialized subjects, and in the physical and social sciences, the humanities, and the professions, especially medicine and dentistry.

Mastery learning strategies have been used successfully in classrooms where the student-teacher ratios have ranged from 20 to 30 to 1 and also in classrooms where the student-teacher ratios approach and surpass 70 to 1! They have even been used effectively to teach the rudiments of such advanced topics as matrix algebra, probability theory, statistics, and mathematical proof to elementary school students.

While there are some definite problems in interpreting the results of some of this research, the following statements still seem fair (Block, 1974).

Intellectual

In general, two to three times as many students have achieved the equivalent of "A"s or "B"s when learning a particular subject by mastery methods rather than by their customary, group-based, non-mastery methods. Thus, if 25% of a group of students earned "A"s or "B"s when learning a particular subject by non-mastery methods, then typically 50 to 75% of a similar group earned "A"s or "B"s when learning the same subject by mastery methods. Furthermore, the data indicate that mastery methods can drastically cut the number of students who receive "C"s, "D"s or "F"s.

There is also a small but growing body of evidence that mastery learning methods can yield better retention of selected topics than non-mastery methods. And a few classroom and experimental studies suggest that they can yield greater transfer of learning than non-mastery approaches. These highly tentative findings seem to hold whether transfer of learning is defined as the ability to apply past learning to the solution of new problems or as the ability to apply past learning to the facilitation of new learning.

Emotional

So far we have considered the effects of mastery learning methods on the intellectual or cognitive aspects of student learning. There is also a growing body of evidence on the impact of these strategies on the emotional or affective aspects.

Available research indicates that mastery methods can yield greater student interest in and more positive attitudes toward the subjects learned than non-mastery approaches. They can also generate increased confidence among students regarding their ability to learn.

Unfortunately, there have been no specific studies yet published of the effects of mastery methods on affective traits such as self-concept and mental health. Related research suggests, however, that mastery methods might help develop or maintain a positive academic self-concept. And more speculative research suggests that they may even help to partially immunize students against *school-induced* mental and emotional disorders.

Learning to Learn

Last, but not least, mastery methods have yielded some evidence that they are helping students learn how to learn. This evidence is primarily anecdotal and impressionistic; it is of three sorts. First, students who have learned by mastery methods have been observed to become more accustomed to the notion that there are many ways to learn in addition to lectures and textbooks. We have been especially intrigued with the extent to which mastery learning students have turned to other students for aid and assistance and have come to exhibit increased cooperation in their learning. Second, mastery learning students have been observed to become more careful and selective in their learning. On the one hand, they do more informal diagnostic-progress testing. Thereby, they gain some measure of quality control over their learning and their study habits. On the other hand, they also spend much more time actively engaged with the material to be learned. They tend not to waste time with extraneous material or in non-learning activities. Third, mastery learning students have been observed to acquire some facility in providing self-reward for their learning. That is, they tend to generate their own learning rewards (e.g., the chance to tutor a peer) rather than relying only on those rewards the teacher might provide.

Work is presently under way to study each of these phenomena in more detail. It may well be that this research will provide an even more compelling case for the classroom use of mastery learning methods than has past research.

References

Block, J. H.: "Operating Procedures for Mastery Learning," in *Mastery Learning: Theory and Practice*. Edited by J. H. Block. New York: Holt, Rinehart and Winston, 1971, 64-76.

Block, J. H.: "New Developments in Mastery Learning in Elementary and Secondary Schools." Paper presented at the annual meeting of the American Educational Research Association, New Orleans, Louisiana, February 28, 1973. (a)

Block, J. H.: "Teachers, Teaching and Mastery Learning," *Today's Education*, *63*, No. 7 (Nov.–Dec. 1973), 30-36. (b)

Block, J. H.: "Mastery Learning in the Classroom: An Overview of Recent Research," in *Schools, Society and Mastery Learning*. Edited by J. H. Block. New York: Holt, Rinehart and Winston, 1974, 28-69.

Bloom, B. S.: "Learning for Mastery," *Evaluation Comment, 1,* No. 2 (1968).

Carroll, J. B.: "A Model of School Learning," *Teachers College Record, 64* (1963), 723-33.

Peterson, P.: "A Review of Research on Mastery Learning Strategies." Unpublished Manuscript. Stockholm: International Association for the Evaluation of Educational Achievement, 1972.

Suggested Readings

Block, J. H. (ed.): *Mastery Learning: Theory and Practice*, New York: Holt, Rinehart and Winston, Inc., 1971.

> This volume brought together for the first time some of the basic ideas underlying mastery learning theory and practice and the best of the relevant supporting research prior to 1971. Part One of the volume consists of a series of articles focusing on mastery learning theory and the implementation of the theory in the classroom. Part Two contains an annotated bibliography of relevant mastery learning research.

Block, J. H (ed.): *Schools, Society, and Mastery Learning*, New York: Holt, Rinehart and Winston, Inc., 1974.

> This volume attempts to explore some of the possible societal implications of teaching for mastery in our schools. Part One of the volume consists of a series of papers designed to acquaint the reader with the present state of the art in mastery learning theory and practice. Part Two explores some of the hypothetical social and economic implications and some of the practical administrative implications of teaching for mastery.

Bloom, B. S.: "Mastery Learning and Its Implications for Curriculum Development," in *Confronting Curriculum Reform*. Edited by E. W. Eisner. Boston: Little, Brown, 1971.

> This paper attempts to explore some of the practical curricular implications of teaching for mastery. The first part of the paper lays out Bloom's ideas on mastery learning. The second part spells out some of the curricular implications of these ideas.

Chapter 2
Planning Your Mastery Strategy: The First Precondition

In the preceding chapter we provided a brief overview of the thinking that led to the development of our "Learning for Mastery" strategy. We also summarized some of the student learning outcomes that have resulted when this thinking has been used in the classroom.

With this overview and summary in mind, let us now turn to a discussion of our suggested mastery learning strategy. The present chapter and Chapter 3 will focus on the planning of this strategy for your classroom. Chapter 4 will concentrate on its implementation. Chapter 5 will answer some questions you might have about teaching for mastery.

How do you go about planning your mastery learning strategy? The answer is, by meeting two important preconditions. First, you will need to define what "mastery" will mean in the subject you have chosen to teach. Then you will need to plan your course so that all of your students can and will attain "mastery." The present chapter will focus on meeting the first of these preconditions; the next chapter will concentrate on meeting the second.

Defining Mastery

We have found the following five step procedure to be very useful for defining mastery.

1. Decide what it is that your textbook expects all of your students to learn. In short, delineate your textbook's instructional objectives. (If you already have these objectives, then begin with step 2.)
2. Put the textbook's instructional objectives down on paper by constructing a course "table of specifications."
3. Revise this table accordingly where the textbook's objectives do not square with your own.

4. Construct a final examination from this table.
5. Set a performance standard on this examination that you will take as being indicative of mastery learning.

Delineating the Textbook's Instructional Objectives

For purposes of this volume we shall assume that you already possess a curriculum and that your problem is how to teach it for mastery. We shall also assume that the bulk of this curriculum is contained in a textbook.[1] In short, throughout the volume we shall assume that you are faced with the problem of teaching for mastery from a textbook. We find that this is the most common problem encountered by the teachers with whom we have worked.

Begin your efforts to delineate the textbook's instructional objectives by determining its major content areas. For this purpose you might peruse the text's table of contents and its index.

The table of contents lists the major sections of the book and also the various chapters within each section. Usually, the major sections are organized around content themes, as are the various chapters. For example, in the table of contents for a grammar book one might find a major section on the mechanics of writing sentences. And within this section he might find chapters on punctuation and capitalization.

The index, on the other hand, gives one some idea of both the major content areas included in the textbook, and more importantly, how thoroughly particular areas are treated. Major content areas, as opposed to minor ones, are frequently referenced and cross-referenced. For example, in one junior high school economics textbook, "Production" seemed to be a major content area. It appeared in the index as follows:

Production, 4
    American, 37-40, 71-72, 86, 173-174
    factors of, 135-136, 138
    Eskimo, 25-28
    Scarcity and, 18, 19
    Soviet Agriculture, 13, 41-42, 116-119, 121, 208, 211, 213
    of consumer goods, 118, 119, 121, 130, 172, 206-209
    goals, 42, 129, 173
    of heavy industry, 40, 42, 115-121, 129, 207, 208, 211, 213
    methods, 122-128
    reforms, 128-131
    See also Capital, Competitions, Dennison Manufacturing Company, Labor Land, Supply and Demand.

---

[1] For purposes of exposition, we shall throughout this volume use the word "textbook" to refer to a single textbook, a set of textbooks, or a portion of a textbook.

The "Industrial Revolution", on the other hand, seemed to be a minor content area. It was indexed:

Industrial Revolution, 116, 145

You may also find it informative to outline the textbook's headings and sub-headings. Most modern textbooks make enormous use of these headings and sub-headings to identify content areas. Most use larger type for the more important headings and sub-headings and smaller type for those of lesser importance. Further, you may want to refer to the teacher's manual for the text. Sometimes these manuals attempt to abstract all of the important major content areas in the textbook and to provide a running chapter-by-chapter summary of them.

Once you have determined the major content areas covered by the textbook, write them on a separate sheet of paper for future reference. Now determine what intellectual operations the textbook expects students to be able to exhibit with each of these areas.

We have found it useful to proceed as follows. Read the text associated with each content area and pay special attention to any questions posed about the area (e.g., questions posed in the text, study or discussion questions at the chapter's end). Now attempt to infer the intent of the textbook's presentation and questions by using Bloom's (1956) *Taxonomy of Educational Objectives: The Cognitive Domain*. This taxonomy contains a set of possible intellectual operations that students might be asked to exhibit with any particular content area (See Table 2-1). Ask, does the textbook intend that the student *know* the material? *comprehend* it? *apply* it? *analyze* it? *synthesize* it? and/or *evaluate* it?

Now, beside each of the textbook's major content areas you have previously listed, write one or more of the following verbs to describe what you believe the textbook expects students to do with the area: "know," "comprehend," "apply," "analyze," "synthesize," "evaluate." Do not be surprised if you use the verbs "analyze," "synthesize," and "evaluate" infrequently. The typical textbook usually requires little more than that the student "know," "comprehend," and "apply" the material presented.

At this point, you have completed the analysis of your textbook. You have identified its major content areas and you have inferred what it expects students to be able to do intellectually with each of these areas. *In short, you have abstracted the textbook's instructional objectives. An instructional objective simply specifies some content to be learned and something the student is expected to be able to do with this content.*

Table 2-1. Bloom's Taxonomy of Educational Objectives*

Operation	Definition and Examples
Knowledge	*The ability to recall or recognize content in a form virtually identical to that in which it was originally presented.* The content may be particular facts, terms, conventions, concepts, rules, generalizations, procedures. For example, the student must remember who discovered America and when or that $E = mc^2$.
Comprehension	*This operation refers to three different abilities: translation, interpretation, and extrapolation.* *Translation involves the ability to change the content presented from one symbolic form to another.* For example, a student must be able to explain the parts of a graph verbally, write a word problem in numerical notation, or change a statement in German to its English equivalent. *Interpretation requires the ability to explain or summarize a body of presented content.* Whereas in translation each part of the content must be changed from form to form, interpretation implies that the student must state the overall meaning of the content. For example, a student must be able to summarize a story. *Extrapolation entails the ability of the learner to go beyond the content presented to determine its probable implications, consequences, or effects given the conditions described.* For example, the student must frequently draw conclusions on the basis of various readings and/or arguments.
Application	*The ability to use the content learned in one situation either to solve a problem or to facilitate learning in a new situation.* For example, the student is asked to use the ideas of addition and subtraction to find an error in a mythical Mr. Jones' checkbook. Or the student is asked to use the principle of "perspective" in learning to draw.
Analysis	*This operation typically refers to two types of abilities: analysis of elements and analysis of relationships.* *The analysis of elements requires that the student be able to break down an aggregate of presented content (e.g., a document an object or a communication) into its constituent parts.* For example, the student is requested to find all of the nouns in a paragraph or to dissect a frog. *The analysis of relationships requires that the student be able to see the relationship between one part of an aggregate of content and the other parts of the aggregate.* For example, the student is asked to trace a statement made early in a novel to an event that occurs later in the novel. Or the student is asked to find the relationship between the use of color in painting and the evocation of emotions.
Synthesis	*The ability to arrange and combine content in such a way as to produce a novel structure, pattern or idea.* At this level, the student must communicate effectively. He also must exercise what

*For a condensed version of Bloom's Taxonomy and more examples see Bloom, Hastings and Madaus (1971) or Gronlund (1970).

Table 2-1. Bloom's Taxonomy of Educational Objectives (cont.)

	some educators would call creative ability. For example, the student is requested to write a theme on "The Three Deadly Enemies of Man" or to put together a class play.
Evaluation	*The ability to make both quantitative and qualitive judgments about the way in which particular elements or aggregates of content meet either external or internal criteria.* The student must make a judgment about the value or worth of something for some purpose.
	The student evaluating on the basis of *internal criteria* is asked to use logical consistency as his evaluation tool. For example, the student must determine whether a writer's conclusions follow from his data or judge whether a computer program is logical. The student evaluating on the basis of *external criteria* is asked to use well-specified criteria provided by experts as his evaluation tool. For example, the student is asked to criticize a research article using Borg and Gall's "Checklist for Evaluating Experimental Research in Psychology and Education." He is also asked to compare the observed outcome with the intended outcome or with the ideal outcome. To illustrate, the student must compare the results of his experiment with the correct results or compare his metal work with the model.

Constructing your Course Table of Specifications

Now put the textbook's instructional objectives down on paper so that you can scrutinize them as a whole. One effective way to do this is to construct what we call a "table of specifications."

A table of specifications is essentially a graphic way of expressing your instructional objectives. The rows of the table designate the major content areas students are expected to learn. Its columns designate the possible intellectual operations students may be expected to exhibit with these content areas. Table 2-2 gives an example of a table of specifications for an eleventh grade chemistry course. This table has been adapted from Bloom, Hastings and Madaus (1971).

Note that in the example, the content areas of interest have been listed down the left hand side of the table. The possible intellectual operations the student might be expected to exhibit with respect to these content areas have been listed across the top. Small x's have then been used to indicate each intellectual operation the student is expected to exhibit with each content area. For example, the circled x indicates that the student is expected to "know" the area of "historical development." The boxed x's indicate he is expected to "know," "comprehend," "apply," and "analyze" the area of "theoretical physics." What are the operations the student is expected to exhibit with respect to the area of "electrochemistry?" If you said "know," "comprehend," and "apply," you're right. How about the area of "measurement"?

Table 2-2. An Example Course Table of Specifications

← – – – – *Possible Intellectual Operations* – – – →

Content Areas	Know	Comprehend	Apply	Analyze	Synthesize	Evaluate
1. Historical Development	(x)					
2. Nature & Structure of Science	x					
3. Nature of Scientific Inquiry	x					
4. Biographies of Scientists	x					
5. Measurement	x	x				
6. Chemical Materials	x	x	x			
7. Chemical Elements	x	x	x	x		
8. Chemical Change	x	x	x			
9. Chemical Laws	x	x	x	x		
10. Energy and Equilibrium	x	x		x		
11. Electrochemistry	x	x	x			
12. Atomic & Molecular Structure	x	x	x	x		
13. Introductory Organic Chemistry	x	x				
14. Chemistry of Life Processes	x					
15. Nuclear Chemistry	x	x	x			
16. Heat & Kinetic Theory	x	x	x	x		
17. Static/Current Electricity	x	x				
18. Magneticism/Electromagneticism	x		x			
19. Theoretical Physics	x	x	x	x		

To construct your own course table of specifications, we suggest you proceed as follows. Take a sheet of graph paper, $8\frac{1}{2}''$ by $11''$ or larger. Down the right hand side of the sheet, copy in pencil your list of the textbook's major areas. Across the top of the sheet write in pencil the verbs "know," "comprehend," "apply," "analyze," "synthesize," and "evaluate."

Now think of each content area as being the beginning of a row that proceeds across the page from left to right. Similarly think of each verb as being the top of a column that proceeds down the page from top to bottom. Take each content area in turn. Proceed along the row corresponding to that area and enter an x in each column headed by the verbs you had written beside that content area when you analyzed the textbook. For example, if beside a particular area you had written the verbs "know," "comprehend," and "analyze," then in the row in your table of specifications corresponding to that content area you would have placed x's in the columns headed up by the verbs "know," "comprehend," and "analyze."

Once you have either x'ed or not x'ed each column in the row, then move to a new content area (i.e., the next row) and repeat the entire procedure. Continue to repeat this procedure with each content area until all the areas (i.e., rows) have been considered.

Try the following example. Suppose that in the analysis of your textbook you have listed three content areas, A, B, and C. Further suppose that beside content area A you had written the verb "know," that beside content area B you had written the verbs "comprehend," "apply," and "analyze," and that beside content area C you had written the verbs "know," "apply," "synthesize," and "evaluate." Take a moment to draw the appropriate table of specifications. Your table should look as follows:

	Know	Comprehend	Apply	Analyze	Synthesize	Evaluate
A	x					
B		x	x	x		
C	x		x		x	x

If you had problems with the construction of this table, you might consult a colleague for help or refer to Bloom, Hastings and Madaus (1971).

Revising your Course Table of Specifications

As you glance over the course table of specifications you have just constructed, a question is likely to come to mind: should I adopt the textbook's instructional objectives for my course or should I add to or subtract from them to obtain a more worthy set of objectives? If you decide that you do want to adopt the textbook's objectives as your own, you are ready to construct your final examination. Skip to page 17. If you decide to alter the textbook's objectives, then read on.

When we have encountered teachers who felt that they could not totally adopt the textbook's objectives as their own, we have encouraged them to modify these objectives to better suit their own tastes. Note that we say *modify*. We have not encouraged the teachers to throw out the textbook's objectives and to start formulating new objectives from scratch. Rather we have suggested that they capitalize on the time they have already spent in analyzing the text and that they keep acceptable objectives and either reformulate or reject the unacceptable ones.

Usually the unacceptable instructional objectives have possessed the following characteristics. They have asked the teacher to emphasize one or more content areas which he deemed unworthy of teaching, or they have asked the student to do far less with a content area than the teacher desired. So in helping teachers to identify potentially unacceptable objectives, we have encouraged them to first identify those major content areas in the text that they believe are most worthy of teaching. We have then suggested that they identify the kinds of intellectual operations that they would like to see the students exhibit relative to these areas. This procedure usually results in the coverage of fewer major content areas than are in the text, but in coverage of these areas in greater depth than the text specifies.

To help you identify the areas that you believe are most worthy of teaching we would suggest two strategies. One of these strategies has proven effective with teachers who have previously taught the subject under consideration. The other has proven effective with teachers who have not previously taught it. You might want to try both.

In the first of these procedures, assemble all of the instructional materials that you may have developed for use in conjunction with the textbook. These materials might include lesson plans, lecture notes, homework assignments, handouts, quizzes, tests, etc. Then "content" analyze these materials, just as you content analyzed the textbook, to determine the major content areas they cover.

Typically, we find that your materials will tend to underemphasize some areas that the textbook has overemphasized. So after the analysis of your materials is completed, return to your subject table of specifications. Then modify its left-hand side by striking out content areas which you believe the textbook has overemphasized. When you strike a content area also erase the x's in the row of the table which correspond to that area.

In the second of these procedures, we suggest that you first estimate the *importance* of each major content area listed in the left-hand side of your course table of specifications. As an aid in your deliberations, obtain opinions of subject matter experts or colleagues regarding the most important content areas for your course. You might find the Bloom, Hastings and Madaus (1971) *Handbook on Formative and Summative Evaluation of Student Learning* to be very useful in this regard. The second half of this book contains chapters written by subject matter experts in various areas: preschool education, language arts, secondary school social studies, art, science, secondary school mathematics, literature, writing, second languages, and industrial education.

Next estimate the *bridgeability* of each content area. Areas which form especially good bridges possess two properties:

1. They build naturally upon content areas to which the students have already been exposed in previous courses and especially upon areas to which they have been exposed in their most recent courses.
2. They clearly link the content areas to which the students have already been exposed to the content areas to which they will likely be exposed in subsequent courses.

Then estimate the *teachability* of each area. Here you are concerned with how much background the student must possess if he is to handle a particular content area in your course. Generally speaking, the more background information and skills required by an area, the lower its teachability. In teaching such areas you will usually find yourself constantly filling gaps in the students' backgrounds, rather than presenting new material.

Now examine the content areas in your course table of specifications. Delete those areas you believe to be unimportant, unbridgeable, and/or unteachable. Then erase the x's in the rows that correspond to these areas.

To help you select more worthy kinds of intellectual operations for your students to exhibit with the content areas you deem worthy of teaching, we would also recommend more procedures. Once again, one of these procedures has proven more effective with teachers who have previously taught the subject under consideration; the other with teachers who have not previously taught it. Again you may want to try your hand at both procedures.

In the first of these procedures, reexamine your assembled instructional materials. But this time analyze the materials in terms of the "intellectual operations" they demand, just as you analyzed the textbook in terms of the intellectual operations it demanded. Once again, pay particular attention to the questions, problems, and exercises posed in these materials with respect to each content area. Ask, do these questions, problems, and exercises require your students to *know* the content area, *comprehend* it, *apply* it, *analyze* it, *synthesize* it or to *evaluate* it?

Now return to your course table of specifications. Think about adding x's to the table to indicate operations with each content area that are demanded by your instructional materials but are not demanded by the textbook. Also think about dropping x's from the table that indicate operations with each content area that are demanded by the textbook but are not demanded by your instructional materials.

In the second procedure, refresh your memory as to the kinds of intellectual operations that are possible with any content area by reviewing Bloom's *Taxonomy*. Then place x's to indicate additional operations you believe your students should be able to exhibit with each major content area in the left-hand column of the course table of specifications.

Constructing your Final Examination

You now have a final version of your course table of specifications which indicates your overall instructional objectives. If you already have a final examination which you feel tests for each of the objectives in this table, i.e., each of the x's, then turn to page 21. If not, construct one.

This test should be *summative* in that it "sums up" student learning in a way that can be used to grade or to certify each student's course performance. (Bloom, Hastings and Madaus, 1971). It also should be criterion-referenced in the sense that it "sums up" student learning with respect to *what* he was expected to learn, i.e., the instructional objectives, rather than to how well he has learned relative to his peers (Block, 1971).

We have found a ten step procedure drawn from the work of Bloom, Hastings and Madaus (1971) and Krathwohl and Payne (1971) to be very useful in constructing such a test.

1. Write on separate 3×5 index cards several test items for each objective designated by an x in your course table of specifications.
2. Be sure that the items you have written fit your objectives.
3. Determine the relative instructional emphasis or importance of each objective.
4. Choose items to test for each objective.
5. Assemble the items according to some systematic plan.
6. Develop a clear set of directions for responding to each type of item. Also develop a sheet upon which the student can record his answers.
7. Establish a scoring procedure that will indicate whether the student has or has not answered each item correctly.
8. Write general directions for the entire test.
9. Try out the test, if possible.
10. Revise your test accordingly.

Since this is not a book on testing, we will only briefly expand on these steps here. We refer the reader to the following excellent source books for a wealth of practical ideas and helpful hints on testing:

For the construction of summative tests see:

> Bloom, B. S., Hastings, J. T. and Madaus, G. F., *Handbook on Formative and Summative Evaluation of Student Learning*. New York: McGraw-Hill, 1971, especially Chs. 4, 7, 8, 9.

For the construction of criterion-referenced testing instruments see:

> Gronlund, N. E., *Preparing Criterion-Referenced Tests for Classroom Instruction*. New York: MacMillan, 1973.

or

> Popham, W. J. *Educational Evaluation*. Englewood Cliffs, New Jersey: Prentice-Hall, 1975. *Evaluating Instruction*. Englewood Cliffs, New Jersey: Prentice-Hall, 1973.

For the writing of test items, the writing of directions and the reproduction of the test see:

> Thorndike, R. L. (ed.), *Educational Measurement*. Second Edition. Washington, D. C.: American Council on Education, 1971, especially Chs. 4, 6, and 7.

Write on separate 3 × 5 index cards several test items for each objective designated by an x in your course table of specifications. We suggest that to start, you try to write what testers call "objective" test items as opposed to essay items, e.g., the short answer form such as completion items, the alternate-choice form such as true-false items, the multiple-choice form, and the matching form.

The chapter by Wesman (1971) in the Thorndike volume provides some excellent examples of each type of item as well as general rules for writing them. The Bloom, Hastings and Madaus (1971) volume provides some helpful hints on writing "objective" items that test for knowledge, comprehension, application, analysis, synthesis and evaluation.

Be sure that the items you have written fit your objectives. That is, be sure that they do indeed test the content areas of interest and that they induce the student to exhibit the appropriate intellectual operations with these areas. For example, if the content area of interest for a particular objective, i.e., a particular x in your table, is Shakespearean plays, then the items should pertain to these plays. And if the operation of interest with this content area is analysis, then the items should test for analysis of Shakespearean plays.

Besides taking care in their construction, one way to help ensure that your items are testing what they are supposed to test is to give them to a colleague or colleagues. Ask these individuals to judge the content area and the operation tapped by each item. Then check their judgments against your own intentions.

Determine the relative instructional emphasis or importance of each objective. One quick, but inexact, way of doing this is to estimate the amount of time that you are likely to devote to the objective during your instruction. More important objectives typically receive more teaching time than less important ones.

Choose items for each objective. Since you are concerned with what objectives each of your students will learn, and not with how well each student will learn relative to his peers, choose your test items accordingly. Choose at least *one* good item to test for *each* of the x's in your subject table of specifications. How many more items you select will depend upon the relative importance or emphasis of the objectives as determined in Step 3. More important objectives should receive more items than less important ones.

We would alert you that there may be practical rub with this procedure, if the number of x's in your table of specifications is large. Your summative test may be too long to administer at a single setting. For example, were we to have selected only 2 items per x for our chemistry table of specifications on page 13, then we would have had a test containing 102 items!

If you encounter this rub, you might want to break your subject table of specifications into two or three smaller tables and construct final examinations for each of these smaller tables. These examinations may then be administered on separate days at the end of the course.

How you break down your subject table of specifications is up to you. We have found it useful to break them down according to content areas. Thus, each of our smaller tables will contain the objectives associated with a particular cluster of related content areas. Typically, we cluster content areas by referring to the textbook's table of contents. We look for the general sections into which the text's various chapters are organized. We then cluster the major content areas covered in the various chapters for each general section. Were we to cluster the content areas covered in this volume, for example, we might cluster the material in Chapter 2 and Chapter 3 because it falls under the general heading of planning a mastery learning strategy.

Assemble the items according to some systematic plan. Try to group objective items of the same type (e.g., multiple choice, true-false, completion, short answer). Also try to group items by content area within a particular type of item. Thus, if one group of multiple choice items tests content area A while a second set of multiple choice items tests content area B, group the A items together and likewise the B items. Lastly, try to arrange the items within a particular content area according to the complexity of the intellectual operations demanded. Thus, "knowledge" items would come first while "evaluation" items would come last. Table 2-3 exemplifies how this plan would be used to assemble items for a 50-item final examination over five hypothetical content areas A, B, C, D, and E.

Table 2-3. Suggested Plan for Assembling Items on a 50 Item Final Examination

Item Types	Content Areas	Item Numbers	Operation	Item Numbers
1. Multiple Choice	A	1 - 10	Knowledge	1 - 6
			Comprehension	7 - 9
			Application	10
	B	11 - 21	Knowledge	11 - 14
			Comprehension	15 - 17
			Application	18
			Analysis	19 - 21
	C	22 - 25	Knowledge	22 - 23
			Comprehension	24 - 25
2. Short-Answer Completion	D	26 - 48	Knowledge	26 - 34
			Comprehension	35 - 37
			Knowledge	26 - 34
			Comprehension	35 - 37
			Application	38 - 40
			Analysis	41 - 44
			Evaluation	45 - 48
	E	49 - 50	Knowledge	49 - 50

Develop a clear set of directions for responding to each type of item. Also develop a sheet upon which the student can record his answers. Procedures for meeting both of these requirements are spelled out in Thorndike and need not detain us here.

Establish a scoring procedure which will indicate whether the student has or has not answered each item correctly. If the items are multiple-choice, true-false, or matching types, a simple "right" answer scoring key will suffice. You might give your key to a colleague with a sample test and ask him to check on the key's clarity. If the items are short-answer completion types, however, a more complex "right" answer key will be required. Your key should list *all* possible acceptable answers. Again you might give your test plus your key to a colleague for review.

Remember, whatever type of scoring key you develop, this key must be absolute. It must indicate as unambiguously as possible whether the student *has* or *has not* answered an item correctly. If your key indicates only that the student *may have* answered the item correctly, then it needs more work. If *you* are unclear about what an acceptable response to a particular item might be, then *your students* may be confused by the item.

Write general directions for the whole test. This is an often overlooked step in the construction of a final examination. The student should be given information concerning such questions as: Should he try all of the items or only try those he feels he knows? Where should he record his answers? How much time will he be given for the test? If completion or short answer items are used, will he be marked on his spelling, grammar, and style?

Try out your test, if possible. A good way to do this involves a little future planning. Suppose that you desire to teach a subject for mastery at some time in the future. If you are now teaching the subject, you might construct your final examination and administer it along with, or in place of, the exam you would normally use to evaluate student learning.

A more cumbersome tryout approach, but one that requires less foresight, would be the following. Entice a handful of students who have already taken the course to sit down with you and to go through the test. Try to obtain students who performed both well and poorly in your course, for both groups of students are likely to pick up misleading or unclear language, terminology, and directions.

Have these students first take the test to establish its time limits. Then go over the test with them. Consider the clarity of its general directions and then the directions for responding to particular items. Ask the students for hints on clarifying directions. Then, consider the clarity of each item in turn. How well is it stated? How well is it keyed? Is the item response format satisfactory? How might the bad items be improved? Attempt to record your students' observations as they work through the test. We have found tape-recording of such sessions to be very useful.

Revise your test accordingly. If you are able to try out your test, then the student tryout information can be used for purposes of revising it. Both the Thorndike (1971) and the Bloom, Hastings, and Madaus (1971) volumes have some excellent suggestions for using this student tryout information for purposes of revision. We would caution you about one point, however. Most books on testing will tell you to drop items that all or almost all of your students answered correctly or incorrectly. They do so because such items do not allow one to make distinctions between the performance of one student and that of another. But mastery learning is not concerned with making these distinctions. Rather it is concerned about what a student has or has not learned. Accordingly, we would recommend that you not drop items that all or almost all of your tryout students answered correctly or incorrectly, *provided* that they do test what you want them to test. Indeed, from a mastery learning perspective it is precisely such items that are most informative about how well you have taught.

Setting a Mastery Performance Standard

You now have your final examination. While this test indicates what your students are expected to learn, it does not indicate how well they must learn it. The final step in defining mastery, then, is the setting of a mastery performance standard, i.e., the setting of a standard of performance on the test that you will be willing to take as being indicative of mastery over your course objectives.

The setting of mastery performance standards is tricky business. As Block (1972) points out, the ideal standard possesses several characteristics that are hard to come by. Rather than trying to set an ideal standard, we suggest that you try to set one with which you feel comfortable. As a rule of thumb, we suggest that you set your standard stringent enough so that if most students attain it, you can say with confidence that your students' learning has improved rather than that your standards have slipped.

In setting your standard we would encourage you to think of mastery in terms of how well you would expect an "A" student to perform with respect to the items which test for *each* course objective. In other words, for each objective we would encourage you to stipulate the number of items that you would expect the "A" students to answer correctly. If a student then answers the stipulated number of items for each objective correctly, i.e., each x in your table, then he may be considered to have mastered your course.

While we have no rule of thumb for suggesting what number of correct items is most reasonable, we would share two observations. First, the more important the objective, the larger the number of correct answers you may want to expect from students. But if you have, say, four to five items for a particular objective, then try not to demand that the student answer all of the items correctly. Answering three out of four or four out of five correctly should suffice. If you have tried out your final examination, then you can obtain at least rough estimates of the number of correct items you want to require. Look at the performance of the top students who took the test. Ask how many of the items for each objective these students were able to answer correctly.

If this approach to the setting of a mastery performance standard is too fine-grained for your purposes, then you might want to consider two coarser standard setting procedures. The first is the easiest to implement but the least informative from the standpoint of providing information for the subsequent revision of your mastery strategy. The second is harder to implement, but more informative.

The first coarse approach utilizes the total score on the final examination rather than an objective-by-objective score. It requires administering the test to a group of students who have been taught, or are being taught, the subject of interest by non-mastery methods. You then determine the total score earned by the "A" students. This "A" score is set as your mastery standard. You are essentially using an existing standard of "A" work under non-mastery learning conditions as your working definition of mastery.

Of course, if you cannot test either former or current students with your final examination, then you can use your own expert judgment or the judgment of your colleagues for selecting a total test score that would be indicative of mastery. You might also use existing state, district or school-wide standards of "A" test performance as your working definition of mastery. Some districts, for example, require that the "A" student score 90% on exams.

For the second coarse approach to setting mastery performance standards, calculate a series of subscores: one subscore for all of the items testing each major content area (i.e., one subscore for each row in your course table of specifications) and one subscore for all of the items testing each type of intellectual operation you expect of your students (i.e., one subscore for all of the items testing each of the columns). Establish what subscore an "A" student taught by non-mastery methods would have attained on the items for each content area and what subscore he would have attained on the items for each operation. Then, as in the objective-by-objective approach, use these stipulated subscores for each content area and for each operation as your working mastery performance standards.

Again, let us emphasize that you must come up with standards that feel right for you. After all, you are the one who must satisfy yourself as to whether mastery approaches to instruction lead to better student learning than your present approach. If you find all three of the preceding approaches to setting standards to be too cumbersome for your purposes, then develop your own. Given the present infant state of the art of setting performance standards, it will be some time before we can provide you with less cumbersome techniques.

References

Block, J. H.: "Criterion-Referenced Measurements: Potential," *School Review, 79* (1971), 289-298.

Block, J. H.: "Toward the Setting of Mastery Performance Standards in Veterinary Medicine," in *Learning Experiences*, Proceedings of the 5th Annual Symposium on Veterinary Medical Education. Edited by J. R. Welser. Athens, Georgia: U. S. Public Health Service, 1972.

Bloom, B. S. *et al.* (eds.): *Taxonomy of Educational Objectives. Handbook I: Cognitive Domain*. New York: McKay, 1956.

Bloom, B. S., Hastings, J. T. and Madaus, G. F.: *Handbook on Formative and Summative Evaluation of Student Learning*. New York: McGraw-Hill, 1971.

Gronlund, N. E.: *Stating Behavioral Objectives for Classroom Instruction*. New York: Macmillan, 1970.

Krathwohl, D. R. and Payne, D. A.: "Defining and Assessing Educational Objectives" in *Educational Measurement*, second edition. Edited by R. L. Thorndike. Washington, D. C.: American Council on Education, 1971, 17-45.

Wesman, A. G.: "Writing the Test Item," in *Educational Measurement*, second edition. Edited by R. L. Thorndike. Washington, D. C.: American Council on Education, 1971, 81-129.

Suggested References

Airasian, P. W. and Madaus, G. F.: "Criterion-Referenced Testing in the Classroom", in *Crucial Issues in Testing*. Edited by Ralph W. Tyler and Richard M. Wolf. Berkeley, California: McCutchan Publishing Company, 1974, 73-87.

> This paper discusses in layman terms some of the main problems and issues associated with criterion-referenced testing.

Bloom, B. S. *et al. Handbook on Formative and Summative Evaluation of Student Learning.* New York: McGraw-Hill, 1971.

> This volume focuses on the role of testing from a mastery learning perspective. One part of the volume shows how to generate a set of instructional objectives and how to test for the attainment of these objectives in a summative manner. The other part indicates how these ideas can be applied in various subject matter areas.

Thorndike, R. L. (ed.): *Educational Measurement,* Second edition. Washington, D. C.: American Council on Education, 1971.

> This volume is a sophisticated, and sometimes very technical, cook-book on testing. Some parts of the volume pertain more to the construction of standardized achievement tests than to the construction of classroom tests, but these parts can be readily adapted to one's purposes. We would highly recommend the following chapters to the general reader: Krathwohl and Payne, "Defining and Assessing Educational Objectives"; Wesman "Writing the Test Item"; and Glaser and Nitko, "Measurement in Learning and Instruction".

Chapter 3
Planning Your Mastery Strategy: The Second Precondition

Now that you have defined what "mastery" will mean in the subject you wish to teach, you are ready to tackle the second major precondition of teaching for mastery. You need to plan how you are going to teach your course for mastery.

We have found the following three step approach to be very useful for this planning.

1. Break your course into a series of "mini-courses," or teaching–learning units.
2. Draw up a table of specifications for each unit.
3. Plan your instruction so as to teach each unit for mastery.
   a. Develop your group-based instructional plan for the unit.
   b. Develop a unit diagnostic-progress test.
   c. Develop supplementary approaches or "correctives" for teaching the unit's material.
   d. Key these correctives to the items on the unit diagnostic-progress test.

Identifying Teaching–Learning Units

In teaching your course, you will be faced with the practical problem that you cannot teach for all of your objectives at the same time. Hence, you need some way of deciding what subset of objectives you will teach at various points in time. We have found the breaking of a course into a number of teaching–learning units useful in this regard. Each of these units will contain only a particular subset of objectives. These units can then be taught so that mastery of each unit's objectives will culminate in mastery of your overall course objectives.

There are many ways we have found useful for identifying teaching–learning units. One way would be to return to your course table of specifications. You might parse this table into small subsets of say 10 or more related objectives, each subset of objectives constituting a teaching–learning unit.

There is a problem with this approach, however. If you happen to pick objectives for a particular unit that are covered in different chapters of the textbook, then you would have to skip around in your textbook teaching. This skipping around might not be rough for you, but it could be rough on your students.

Therefore we propose that you use the chapters of the textbook as your teaching–learning units. Useful teaching–learning units cover about two weeks' worth of objectives. So if your textbook chapters take about 10 to 14 days to cover, then each chapter may form a teaching–learning unit. If a particular chapter requires only a couple of days to teach, then it may be combined with a prior or a subsequent chapter to form a unit of reasonable length. Or if a chapter requires many weeks to cover, then it may be subdivided to form several units.

Constructing Unit Tables of Specifications

Now extract the instructional objectives of each unit just as you extracted the textbook's overall objectives. This time you will want to focus on the various content *elements* which comprise the unit and the intellectual operations the textbook expects students to exhibit with these elements.

Begin by identifying the new content elements that are introduced in the chapter, chapters, or parts of a chapter that make up the unit. This content will often be highlighted through the use of different type, color-codes, boxes, or underlinings. It will also often be summarized at the end of the chapters and in your teacher's manual. You may also want to "content" analyze any other instructional materials you have developed for use in conjunction with the chapter or chapters of interest.

Usually, these new content elements will take the form of *terms, facts, concepts, principles,* or *procedures.* Table 3–1 defines and illustrates what we mean by each of these forms. As you look through each unit's materials, use Table 3–1 to identify the unit's content elements.

Once you have identified the content elements in a unit, then attempt to infer what intellectual operations the textbook (and any associated instructional materials) expects students to exhibit with each element. And, again, attempt to categorize these operations in terms of Bloom's *Taxonomy.* Determine whether the instructional materials require the student to *know* each element, *comprehend* it, *apply* it, *analyze* it, *synthesize* it, or *evaluate* it.

Table 3–1 Content Elements Commonly Found in Instructional Materials

Element	Definition and Examples

Terms

The new or special vocabulary words or phrases which are introduced in the materials. Typically these words and phrases will be defined in the materials or in a glossary or summary at their end. In this volume, for example, "tables of specifications", "correctives", and "diagnostic-progress test" would all be considered terms.

Facts

Particular bits of information in the materials that may be regarded as important. These bits of information are usually of three types:

Additional information about particular terms. For example, if the term of importance is "hare," then the definition might include words or phrases that indicate the hare is long-eared, short-tailed, burrowing mammal, or a member of the family *Leporidae*. One of the interesting facts (added information) about the hare is that the tortoise beat the hare in the famous race.

Additional information about people and/or places. For example, facts about Antoine Lavoisier might include that he was born in 1743, that he was French, he was a chemist, or that he is regarded as the father of modern chemistry. A fact about Sherwood Forest might be that it housed Robin Hood or that it stands in England.

Additional information about events. For example, facts about the Battle of Bull Run might include that it was a battle of the American Civil War, that it was fought in Virginia, that the Confederates defeated the Union forces, that it was fought in 1861, and that a second battle was fought at Bull Run in 1862.

Concepts

"Super" terms used to organize terms and facts in the materials which are similar in some respects. The "super" terms are usually of two types (Gagné, 1974):

Concrete concepts are used to describe similarities among the attributes of physical, tangible objects or entities. For example, if the terms and facts of interest characterize balls, then the concrete concepts of *smoothness*, *roundness*, or *color* might be used to group these terms and facts.

Abstract or defined concepts are used to describe hypothetical or intangible objects or entities. For example, if the terms and facts of interest characterize several kinds of democracies, then the abstract concept of *form of representative government* might be used to group the terms and facts.

Principles

The major organizational ideas, patterns, and or schemes in the materials which describe the relationships which exist among several concepts. These are also often called rules or generalizations, and are typically of two types (Gagné, 1974):

Lower-order principles relate two or more concepts to each other. For example, if the concepts of interest were supply and demand, then the lower-order principle might be that *as demand increases, supply increases.* Or if the concepts were interest rates and capital investment, then the lower-order principle might be that *high interest rates reduce capital investment.*

Table 3–1 (cont.)

Element	Definition and Examples
Principles (cont.)	*Higher-order* principles make use of two or more lower-order principles. Suppose, for example, that one lower-order principle is that truth is more desirable than justice in a court case and another lower-order principle is that justice is more desirable than logic. The higher order principle would be that truth is more desirable than logic in a court case.
Procedures	*A series of steps (generally in a sequence) that students must be able to perform in or with the instructional materials.* These procedures are based on a series of underlying principles, but sometimes these principles are unknown to the student. For example, a procedure must be learned to take the square-root of a number, to write a business letter, or to conduct a laboratory procedure.

You now have the instructional objectives for each unit. You have identified the new content elements to be learned in each unit and the intellectual operations that students are expected to exhibit with these content elements. Accordingly, cast these objectives into unit tables of specifications. These tables will allow you to glance readily over each unit's objectives as a whole, just as the course table of specifications allowed you to glance readily at your course objectives as a whole.

We would suggest that you construct each of your unit tables just as you constructed your course table of specifications (see page 13), *with one exception*. We strongly suggest that you cluster content elements in each unit that seem to fit together and that you list content elements by cluster down the left-hand side of each unit table. In each cluster, list first a procedure or related procedures, then principles related to this procedure or these procedures, then concepts related to these principles and then terms and facts related to these concepts. If you have no procedures in a cluster, then begin your list with a principle or related principles. And if you have no principles (no pun intended), then begin with a concept or related concepts. For an even more complete listing of various content elements within a particular cluster, you might want to list higher-order principles before the lower-order ones; abstract concepts before concrete; and facts involving particular terms before the terms themselves. Any content elements in each unit that do not fit any content clusters can then be listed at the bottom of the unit table. Table 3–2 gives an example of a unit table of specifications in which content elements have been clustered.

Now correlate these unit tables against your course table of specifications. Somewhere in the unit tables you should be able to find each of the objectives in your course table. If you cannot locate particular course objectives in any of the unit tables, you will have to write them in to those unit tables which seem most appropriate. If you decide to adopt the textbook's objectives as your own, you should not face this situation too often. If you decided to modify the textbook's objectives to better suit your purposes, you will encounter it more frequently.

Table 3-2 A Clustered Unit Table of Specifications

Operations

	Know	Comprehend	Apply	Analyze	Synthesize	Evaluate
Content Cluster 1						
Procedure A	x	x	x			
Principle B	x	x	x			
Concept C	x	x	x			
Concept D	x					
Fact E	x					
Fact F	x	x				
Term G	x					
Term H	x					
Content Cluster 2						
Concept I	x	x				
Fact J	x	x	x			
Fact K	x					
Term L	x					
Other Content Elements						
Principle M	x					
Fact N	x					
Term O	x					

Planning Your Unit Instruction

So far you have decided what material, textbook and otherwise, you are going to cover to reach your overall course objectives, and you have allocated this material into convenient teaching–learning units. You must now decide how you will actually teach each unit's material for mastery. Clearly if *how* you teach each unit is unsatisfactory, then your students will have little chance to acquire *what* you are trying to teach.

Planning the Group-Based Instruction

The first step in planning your unit instruction is to decide how you will present each unit to your students as a group and involve them in its learning. *We would suggest that you go about planning your group-based instruction for each unit as usual.* The tools you are now going to develop should, when implemented, give you some specific information about the adequacy of this plan. If necessary, you can then use this information to make your group-based instructional plan even more effective in the future.

Constructing a Unit Diagnostic-Progress Test

The second step in planning your instruction for each unit is to construct a unit diagnostic-progress test. Unlike your final examination, this test will form an integral part of the unit's teaching–learning process. It will be administered at the end of the unit's group-based instruction to monitor the effectiveness of the teaching–learning process. Its results will indicate how each student's learning *is changing* relative to the unit's instructional objectives (Airasian, 1971). Hence, if all of your students are changing as desired, then both they and you can move on in the teaching–learning process with confidence. But if some students are not changing as desired, then you can still intervene to get the process back on track for these students.

The ideal diagnostic-progress test will be brief so that it does not take up inordinate amounts of instructional time. It will also be prescriptive. By this we mean it should provide information or feedback to both the students and you regarding *where* the student might, if necessary, start his restudying and review of particular material.

To construct a unit diagnostic-progress test which approaches this ideal, we suggest that you proceed as follows. For every objective in the unit table of specifications, construct several items. We would suggest that you write these items on 3 × 5 cards. Again try writing "objective" rather than "essay" type items, especially alternate choice or multiple choice "objective" items. This will save testing and scoring time and allow students to score their own tests.

Next, decide how much instructional time you can comfortably give up for diagnostic-progress testing on the unit. Fifteen to twenty minutes should usually be enough, though some teachers have even allowed thirty minutes. Remember, you do not want to spend so much time testing that the testing gets in the way of your teaching.

Then estimate how many test items your students can reasonably be expected to answer in the testing time allowed. We allow on the average about 45 to 60 seconds per item. So if we have twenty minutes for testing, then our diagnostic-progress test would contain a maximum of twenty to twenty-five items.

Now select the particular items which will comprise your test. Choose from the items you have constructed, one best item and a "back-up" item to test for *each* objective in your unit table of specifications. Save the "back-up" items and store them for future use. Then proceed to assemble the best items you have selected into a test.

We highly recommend the following assembly scheme (see Table 3-3). Group all of the items that test for the objectives associated with each cluster of content elements in your unit table. Within each of these groups of items list first the items that test for "knowledge", then those that test for "comprehension", etc. Now assemble your test, one group of items after another. You may put the items that test for the objectives unassociated with any content element clusters in your unit table at the end of the test.

Table 3-3. Proposed Assembly Scheme for Clustering Diagnostic-Progress Test Items

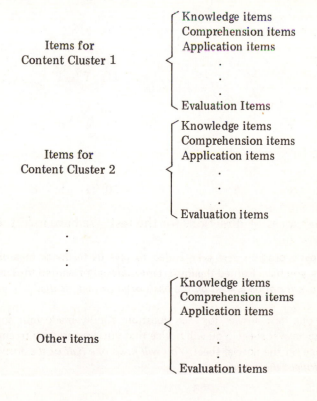

This manner of assembling your test may seem cumbersome right now. But as you will see in the next chapter, it will prove very useful in guiding the review and restudy of students whose unit diagnostic-progress test results indicate that such activities are necessary.

Now prepare an answer sheet and scoring key for the test. Our scoring keys have been fairly traditional. We have simply marked the correct answers on a copy of the unit answer sheet. But our answer sheets have been untraditional. We suggest you use a double answer sheet (see Table 3-4). The student can then mark his answer to each question twice—once on one half of the sheet and once on the other. Once corrected, this sheet can be torn in half. The student can keep one half, thereby gaining information about the effectiveness of his learning on the unit. You can collect the other half, thereby gaining information about the effectiveness of your unit group-based instructional plan.

Table 3-4. A Sample Portion of a Unit Diagnostic-Progress Test Answer Sheet

Name_____	Name_____
Directions: Circle the *Letter* of the correct answer.	*Directions*: Circle the *Letter* of the correct answer.
1. a b c d	1. a b c d
2. a b c d	2. a b c d
.	.
.	.
.	.
10. T F	10. T F
11. T F	11. T F
.	.
.	.
15. a b c	15. a b c
.	.
.	.
.	.
20. a b c	20. a b c

Lastly develop a set of directions for the test. We have used the following:

This diagnostic progress test is intended to give us feedback regarding how successfully you have learned the important material presented thus far in this course. *You will not be graded on the basis of your test results.*

Select the one best answer for each question. Kindly mark your answer on the separate answer sheet. You will notice that you are required to enter your answer twice on the answer sheet. *You will keep one half of the answer sheet and I will collect the other.*

As you can see, these directions serve two purposes. They reemphasize to the student that the diagnostic-progress test results will not be used for grading. Rather, they will be used to provide information about the effectiveness of the on-going teaching-learning process. The directions also point out that the test is designed to provide this information to the student as well as the teacher.

Developing Unit Correctives

You now have your group-based plan of instruction for each unit and a unit diagnostic-progress test that can be used to monitor the effectiveness of this plan in terms of your students' learning. The last step you need to take in planning how to teach the unit for mastery is to come up with some supplementary approaches for teaching the unit. We call such approaches "correctives."

Why do you need these "correctives?" You are doing what a good teacher always does—planning for a possible contingency. No matter how good your group-based plan may be for a particular unit, it may not be good enough to meet totally the learning requirements of some of your 25 to 30 students. Some students may fail to learn particular material in the unit. You need, then, some way of capitalizing on the time and effort you have put into your group-based instruction for the unit so as to get this particular material through to these students. Correctives serve this purpose.

We have one cardinal rule for the selection of correctives for a particular teaching-learning unit. *They must teach the same material as does your group-based plan for the unit, but they must do so in ways that differ from this plan.* In other words, the correctives should not only supplement the group-based instruction, but provide some alternatives to it. Since the point of most group-based plans of instruction is to *present* the material to be learned and to *involve* students in its learning, this rule means the following. *Your correctives should present the unit's material in ways that differ from the way your group-based plan will present it. They should also involve students in learning the unit's material in ways that differ from the way your group-based plan will involve them.*

Let us suggest some of the general types of correctives we have found to be useful in our work. In the initial stages of your mastery learning program we would encourage you to give our correctives a try. Then as you become more sophisticated in the use of correctives, you may wish to develop your own.

Our General Types of Correctives

We would characterize each of our general types of correctives in terms of (1) whether they can be used for *individual* learners or a *group* of learners and (2) whether they focus on alternative ways of *presenting* the material to be learned or on alternative ways of *involving* the student in learning this material.

Alternative Textbooks. Alternative textbooks are what we call "individual presentational" correctives. They are used to give the student a different slant on the textbook material relevant to each of the unit's objectives.

For each important content element in the unit we identify alternative treatments in other textbooks. In selecting these alternative treatments we try to obtain presentations of each content element that are different from one another and from the textbook's presentation. We then note the pages in each alternative text where one might find a treatment of the particular content elements in the unit.

Workbooks. Workbooks are also "individual presentational" correctives. They are used to give the student more familiarity with the textbook material for each unit.

For each important content element in the unit we identify the pages on which the content element is treated in the workbook that accompanies the text (or in related workbooks). We then note these pages for future reference by students.

Flashcards. Flashcards are yet another "individual presentational" corrective. They are used to give the student repeated exposure to the particular terms, facts, concepts, and principles covered in the unit.

For all of the important terms, facts, etc., we prepare a deck of cards (usually out of 3×5 note cards). On one side of each card we list the appropriate term, fact, etc. On the other side, we provide a corresponding definition, explanation, or illustration. We then number the cards for future reference so that each student can readily select just those cards from the deck that he requires.

Reteaching. Reteaching is a "group presentational" corrective. It is used to reteach particular material in a unit to a group of students who had difficulty with this material.

When using "reteaching" as a corrective procedure, it is especially important that the teacher make the reteaching as different as possible from the original group-based instruction. There are two ways in which this can be done. First, the teacher can plan on reteaching the material himself, taking care to make use of different examples, illustrations and/or formats. For example, if the teacher originally plans to present the unit's material in a lecture format, he can plan to reteach the problematic portions of the lecture using a discussion format. Second, the teacher can plan to have someone else do the reteaching. We have found it effective to have a student who initially mastered the problematic material of interest do the reteaching.

Audio-Visual Aids and Materials. A-V materials are another type of "group presentational" correctives. They are used to teach the unit's material to a group of students, but to do so in a highly visual *and* auditory manner. We have found two classes of audio-visual materials useful in our work. One class has included existing audio-visual materials such as films, filmstrips, models, video-tapes, and slides (with accompanying sound). The other class consists of teacher made audio-visual materials such as graphs, overheads, outlines on blackboards, photographs, and concrete props that complement the verbal presentation of the material of interest.

A good reference source for teachers about existing audio-visual materials is the *Mini-Catalog of Instructional Systems and Materials* published by the Technical Applications Project, 8660 Miramar Road, Suite M, San Diego, California (92126). Another good reference source on existing audio-visual materials is the ERIC Clearinghouse on Information Resources, Center for Research and Development in Teaching, Stanford University, Stanford, California (94305). The best source of which we know for the construction and classroom use of teacher prepared audio-visual materials are the *Proceedings* of the various national Audio-Tutorial Conferences which began at Purdue University in connection with the work of Samuel N. Postlethwait, Professor of Biology.

Token Economies. A token economy is what we call an "individual involvement" corrective. It is a classroom system which attempts to involve the student in learning the material of interest by giving him token or points in exchange for learning. These tokens (e.g., play money) or points can then be exchanged for something the student desires, usually material rewards (e.g., prizes, food) or the chance to engage in some preferred activity (e.g., "free" time or a hobby).

Token economies are relatively simple for the teacher to manage. Before a teacher develops a token economy system, however, we would suggest that he consult the following sources for a fuller discussion of the concept coupled with step-by-step implementation plans.

> Givner, A., and Graubard, P. S. *A Handbook of Behavior Modification for the Classroom*. New York: Holt, Rinehart and Winston, 1974.

> Krasner, L. and Krasner, M. "Token Economies and Other Planned Environments," in *Behavior Modification in Education*. The Seventy-second Yearbook of the National Society for the Study of Education (Part I). Chicago: University of Chicago Press, 1973.

Academic Games. Academic games are what we call "group involvement" correctives. These games attempt to involve a group of students who have similar learning problems in solving these problems not for their own sake but to gain the goal or purpose of the game.

We first attempt to modify or to adapt existing games that bear on the problems of interest. If such games are not available, then we attempt to develop our own.

Since most teachers will not have time to develop their own games, we suggest that you write the Center for Social Organization of Schools, Johns Hopkins University, Baltimore, Maryland (21218) for more information about existing academic games that may be modified to suit your purposes.

Group Affective Exercises. Group affective exercises are also "group involvement" correctives. In these exercises, students who are having similar learning problems are asked to experience the problematic material not at the intellectual level, but at an emotional one. For example, they might be asked to feel what it is like to be a number, a part of speech, or a protagonist in a novel.

There are no hard and fast rules for the development of these exercises, but the literature abounds with examples of them. If you desire to learn more about the use of these exercises in the classroom you might consult the following sources.

Brown, G. I. *Human Teaching for Human Learning*. New York: The Viking Press, 1971.

Brown, G. I. *et al. The Live Classroom*. New York: Viking Press, 1975.

Castillo, G. A. *Left-Handed Teaching*. New York: Praeger Publishers, 1974.

Schrank, J. *Teaching Human Beings*. Boston: Beacon Press, 1972.

You might also write the Confluent Education Program at the Graduate School of Education, University of California, Santa Barbara, Ca. (93106) or the Center for Humanistic Education at the School of Education, University of Massachusetts, Amherst, Mass. (01002).

Programmed Instruction. Programmed instruction is what we would call an "individual presentational/involvement" corrective. Students with particular learning problems can be referred to the appropriate pages in the programmed text. There they will usually find a simplified presentation of the problem material. They will also find continuous positive reinforcement for their learning of this material.

To use a programmed textbook, we simply note the pages upon which the text covers each element of the important material in the unit. We then list these pages for future use by the students.

Since it is unlikely that you will have the time to develop your own programmed instructional materials, we would suggest that you gather materials that have already been developed. Fortunately, there are a wide variety of these materials currently available. To locate some of these materials we suggest that you write to:

The Technical Applications Project
8660 Miramar Road, Suite M
San Diego, California 92126

ERIC Clearinghouse on Information Resources
Center for Research and Development in Teaching
Stanford University, Stanford, California 94305

Tutoring. Tutoring is also an "individual presentational/involvement" corrective. The able tutor seems to present problematic materials to the student in a variety of modes almost effortlessly. And he slides easily from involving the student in one way to involving him in another when learning encounters a snag.

In our own work, we have tended to use peers as tutors. We simply solicit students who have mastered particular material to teach that material to classmates who are having difficulty with it. However, some teachers with whom we have worked have preferred to use former students as tutors. That is, they have encouraged cross-age tutoring rather than same-age tutoring. And still other teachers with whom we have worked have used adults (e.g., retired persons, parents, volunteers, etc.). Whether you use classmates, former students, or adults, suffice it to say that tutoring is a powerful, all-purpose corrective. If you desire to obtain some idea of the work going on in research on tutoring, we highly recommend that you examine the following sources:

Bloom, S. "Effects of Tutorial Programs in the Urban School Setting." Washington, D. C.: National Institute of Education, in press.

Moore, C. A. "Tutoring, Dyadic Interaction and Interpersonal Processes". Unpublished bibliography, 1971. (Ms. Moore is a research associate at Educational Testing Service, Division of Psychological Studies, Princeton, New Jersey)

Small-group Study Sessions. Small-group study sessions are considered to be a "group presentation/involvement" strategy. They are essentially a sophisticated group approach to tutoring.

In these sessions, three to four learners get together to discuss their learning problems. We try to be sure that each student in a group has very different learning problems than his partners. This way each student has learned some material that he can teach to the other members in the group; he can tutor his peers as well as be tutored by them.

In a typical session, the students first identify the diagnostic-progress test items with which they have had difficulty. They then go over each of these items as follows. One student who has answered the item of interest correctly will explain the material tested by the item and give his reasons for choosing the answer he did choose. The floor is then open for discussion about the material tested by the item and about the correct answer to the item.

Table 3-5 provides a quick summary of each of the general types of correctives we have discussed in terms of whether they are individual or group correctives. It also indicates whether they focus on presenting the unit's material and/or involving students in its learning in a different way than typically will the group-based plan.

Table 3-5. A Summary of Our General Types of Correctives

Corrective	Individual	Group	Presentation	Involvement
Alternative Textbooks	✓		✓	
Workbooks	✓		✓	
Flashcards	✓		✓	
Reteaching		✓	✓	
Audio-Visual* Materials		✓	✓	
Token Economies	✓			✓
Academic Games		✓		✓
Group* Affective Exercises		✓		✓
Programmed Instruction	✓		✓	✓
Tutoring	✓		✓	✓
Small Group Study Sessions		✓	✓	✓

*These correctives might also be used on an individual basis in some situations.

Generally speaking, of the types of correctives listed here, we have found the *small-group study sessions* to be the most versatile for primary, secondary and college students. This type of corrective seems to offer all the advantages of a tutorial approach to instruction, yet enables more than one student to be tutored at a time. We have also tended to find that the *individual* correctives listed here seem to be more effective with older students than younger ones. We believe that this may be because younger students have not yet developed the sense of autonomy and responsibility that is typically required to use the individual correctives on their own. Lastly, we have tended to find that the *involvement* correctives listed here seem to be more popular with and effective among students than the presentation correctives. We believe that this is because most group-based plans of instruction tend to focus primarily on presenting the material and ignore involving students in its learning. We are presently exploring these observations and especially the central role of involvement in school learning.

Developing Your Own Correctives

Earlier we suggested that you might want to develop your own correctives after you have had some experience in teaching for mastery. We will now sketch some ideas for this purpose. The material to follow is more challenging than the previous material in this chapter. But we believe that its study will prove fruitful.

The key to developing your own correctives for a unit is some understanding of the nature of your group-based approach to the unit. Once you know how your group-based approach will present the unit's material and involve students in its learning, then you can design your correctives to present this same material in other manners and to involve students in other ways.

Different instructional psychologists have different approaches to the analysis of a group-based instructional plan. We would propose that you proceed as follows:

First, determine how your group-based plan will go about *presenting* the unit's material by asking the following questions:

1. What learner sense modality or modalities does my group-based plan demand—auditory, visual, and/or tactile?[1] Lectures, class presentations and discussions, for example, rely on your students' auditory sense mode. Reading, films, overheads, graphics, flashcards, boardwork, and demonstrations would play on their visual sense mode. Concrete learning experiences (e.g., Cuisenaire rods, building models, finger painting, physical education) and interpersonal exercises (e.g., sensitivity exercises) play on their tactile sense mode. Most group-based plans of instruction rely heavily on students' auditory sense modes, less heavily on their visual modes and practically not at all on their tactile modes. The only exception to this generalization seems to occur in the pre-school, the kindergarten, and the early primary grades, where the tactile sense mode is becoming more frequently emphasized.

2. What primary mental abilities does my group-based instruction tap? In particular, does it require verbal comprehension or ability, word fluency, numerical ability, spatial ability or short-term memory ability (Harris and Harris, 1974)? Each of these abilities may be thought of as a kind of intelligence that your group-based plan will demand of your students (Thurstone, 1963). Most of your students will likely be gifted with one or more of these intelligences, though they may not be gifted with respect to the particular intelligences demanded by your group-based plan.

[1]One could, of course, have a group-based plan that plays upon the olfactory and/or gustatory sense modalities. For example, perhaps one of the most powerful learning experiences we ever had was in science when our group-based instruction taught us about hydrogen sulfide. We can still vividly recall the "rotten egg" smell.

a. *Verbal comprehension or ability* (what some teachers commonly call intelligence) will be required of students if your instruction uses a large and varied vocabulary or if it asks them to induce what they are to learn from meaningful, organized, pictorial representations (e.g., film, graphs, pictures) or verbal statements (e.g., reading assignments, lectures, discussions).

b. *Word fluency* will be required if your instruction demands that students constantly make use of whatever vocabulary they have whether it be large or small (e.g., to respond to questions in class, to take part in discussions, to write essays). Some students can possess a great verbal comprehension but they are unable to express themselves fluently. Other students can express themselves fluently but only within a limited vocabulary range.

c. *Numerical ability* will be required if your instruction demands that students compute or use numbers so as to learn about something else. For example, if you ask your students to calculate a value in an equation or formula so as to learn about the equation or formula, or to count the couplets in a poem so as to learn about the poem, then you are playing on their numerical ability.

d. *Spatial ability* will be required if your instruction asks students to think in two and three dimensions in order to learn. On the one hand, you may ask your students to take a three-dimensional instructional presentation and reduce it to essentially two dimensions. For example, in chemistry or physics the student must often draw the experimental apparatus to follow the discussion.

On the other hand, you may ask your students to take two-dimensional instructional materials and to think about them as if they were three-dimensional. For example, you may ask students to construct a setting from a book's description or a picture; to construct a relief map from a topographical map; to carry out manipulations of concrete objects by following along with a demonstration, film, or overhead.

e. *Short-term memory ability* will be required if your instruction bombards students with many pieces of information in a relatively short period of time and expects that they take in all of this information for later use. For example, you may begin a class period with a long list of information about particular Civil War battles (e.g., time, location, general, victor) and expect them to have this information on tap as you begin your discussion of the spread of the war shortly into the period. Some students possess the capacity to store enormous amounts of information for a brief period of time. Others do not. Some of the information presented literally runs in one ear and out the other.

We typically find that most group-based plans of instruction in all types of courses rely heavily on students' verbal comprehension, word fluency, and short-term memory abilities. Numerical ability tends to be used most often in the group-based plans of instruction for mathematics and science courses. Spatial ability is most frequently used in mathematics, science, art (including industrial arts), and physical education courses.

Once you have determined what sense modalities and primary mental abilities you believe your group-based plan of instruction will tap, then write these modalities and abilities down for future use. Now attempt to determine how your group-based plan will go about *involving* students in learning what they are expected to learn. For this purpose, we suggest that you ask the following questions.

1. What kinds of intrinsic or internal incentives for learning does my group-based plan of instruction tap? These incentives play on the students' background (prior experiences, interests, concerns) and on their desire to continually seek out, rather than to avoid, stimulation and excitement.

In particular, we recommend that you ask questions about your group-based plan such as these:

    a. What prior student learnings does it tap?
    b. What student interests and/or concerns does it build upon?
    c. What novel situations or problems does it pose?
    d. What challenging but *clear* situations or problems does it pose for which there is an answer? More than one possible answer? No answers?
    e. What challenging but *ambiguous* situations or problems does it pose for which there is an answer? More than one possible answer? No answers?

In other words, ask how your group-based plan stimulates and excites your students to explore the material presented and how it continually piques their curiosity to learn more.

2. What kinds of extrinsic or external incentives for learning does my group-based plan of instruction offer? Whereas intrinsic incentives for learning are built into the learner's constitution and need only be given some avenues for expression in your group-based plan, extrinsic incentives are given to the learner under the assumption that without them he would not learn. In short, they are reasons for learning that are given to the learner, but which are not built into his constitution.

Table 3-6 indicates some of the types of external incentives that have been used in the classroom to encourage student involvement. Almost any book on behavioral modification in the classroom contains many more examples.

Table 3-6. Some External Incentives for Learning

Material	Social	Learner Preferred Activities
Grades	Teacher Praise	Time for "Break" (Free Time)
Stars	oral	Use of Private Study Booth
Prizes	written	Sitting Next to Friend
Money	Peer Praise	Use of Typewriter
Tokens	Public Recognition	Being a "Teacher Assistant"
Food	class	Time for Hobbies
	school	Use of Library or Media Center
	community	Leading a Group Game
		Going to Recess
		Going on a Field Trip
		Drawing Pictures
		Playing a Game

a. *Material incentives* are tangible incentives that the student can earn. Once they are earned they can then be displayed or consumed to satisfy one *immediate* need or concern (e.g., hunger, the need to achieve, anxiety) or they can be exchanged for other goods, services or privileges to satisfy another pressing need or concern. They can also be saved to satisfy a more *distant* need or concern.

b. *Social incentives* may be tangible or intangible incentives that the student can earn. The importance of these incentives lies less in the *form* that the incentive is given (e.g., praise) but in *who* gives the incentive. Material incentives indicate a personal accomplishment; social incentives indicate that a personal accomplishment is prized by someone else.

c. *Learner-preferred activity incentives* are also tangible or intangible incentives that the student can earn. They represent activities in which the student would be likely to engage were he free to choose and had a wide range of activities from which to select (Premack, 1965). In using these incentives, the teacher simply observes what a particular student or a group of students like to do and then says, in effect, "I'll allow you to do what you like to do, if you will learn what I want you to learn."

Once you have determined what internal and external incentives for involvement you believe your group-based plan of instruction will offer, then write them down on the same sheet that you wrote the sense modalities and abilities. You are now ready to develop your own correctives. You have some idea of both how your group-based plan will present the material students are expected to learn and how it will involve them in its learning.

Check the list of sense modalities, primary mental abilities, and incentives you believe are demanded by your group-based plan of instruction for the unit. Note the modalities, abilities, and incentives that your plan seems to neglect. Then develop correctives which can teach the unit's material relying on these neglected modalities, abilities and incentives.

Suppose, for example, that your group based plan relies primarily on the auditory sense mode, verbal ability, and external kinds of incentives. To be specific, suppose you planned to lecture, to use virtually no graphics, overheads, etc., and to use social incentives for learning, particularly praise. You might then search for correctives that would rely more heavily on your students' visual and tactile sense modes; would emphasize non-verbal abilities such as spatial or numerical abilities; and would emphasize internal incentives for learning and/or other types of external incentives. You might, for example, plan to illustrate particular points in your lectures using models, demonstrations or experiments, and give your students a chance to study these illustrations with a friend. Here you would play on your students' visual sense mode, their spatial ability, and learner preferred external incentives for learning. Or you might ask your students to build for themselves, using rulers, a concrete model to represent particular points in your lecture and let them build their model in any way that interests them. In this case you would play on their visual and tactile sense modes, their spatial and numerical abilities, and internal incentives for learning. The alternative instructional possibilities are almost endless.

Keying the Correctives to the Unit Diagnostic-Progress Test

Once you have developed your unit correctives, then the final step in planning how to teach each unit for mastery is to key each unit's correctives to the unit diagnostic-progress test. This will help to ensure that a student will not select a particular corrective for a unit only to find that the corrective really does not cover the material of interest.

For this purpose, we recommend that you develop a "corrective sheet" which can be given to students after the diagnostic-progress test results are in. This sheet would simply indicate the number of each item on the test and the objective tested by each item. Beneath each objective it would then list the particular correctives from which the student might choose to review and restudy the material in the unit relevant to this particular objective.

References

Airasian, P. W.: "The Role of Evaluation in Mastery Learning," in *Mastery Learning: Theory and Practice.* Edited by J. H. Block. New York: Holt, Rinehart and Winston, 1971, 77-88.

Gagné, R. M.: *Essentials of Learning for Instruction*. Hinsdale, Illinois: The Dryden Press, 1974.

Harris, M. L. and Harris, C. W.: *A Structure of Concept Attainment Abilities.* Madison, Wisconsin: Wisconsin Research and Development Center for Cognitive Learning, 1973.

Premack, D.: "Reinforcement Theory," in *Nebraska Symposium on Motivation*. Edited by D. Levine. Lincoln: University of Nebraska Press, 1965.

Thurstone, L. L.: "Testing Intelligence and Aptitudes," in *Contributions to Modern Psychology*, Second Edition. Edited by D. Dulany, Jr. *et al.* New York: Oxford University Press, 1963, 49-60.

Suggested Readings

Airasian, P. W.: "The Role of Evaluation in Mastery Learning," in *Mastery Learning: Theory and Practice*. Edited by J. H. Block. New York: Holt, Rinehart and Winston, 1971.

> The type of unit diagnostic-progress tests we have asked you to develop in this chapter are technically known as "formative" evaluation instruments. In this paper, Airasian spells out some of the central properties of formative tests and develops some procedures for constructing them. The type of formative tests that Airasian builds are even more prescriptive than the diagnostic-progress tests we asked you to construct.

Bloom, B. S., Hastings, J. T., and Madaus, G. F.: *Handbook on Formative and Summative Evaluation of Student Learning*. New York: McGraw-Hill, 1971.

> Chapter 6 of this volume spells out in even greater detail than Airasian's paper how to construct formative evaluation instruments.

Gagné, R. M.: *Essentials of Learning for Instruction*. Hinsdale, Illinois: The Dryden Press, 1974.

> This is a useful little volume for teachers on how to design their instruction to attain particular kinds of learning outcomes. The volume should be especially useful as you wrestle with the problem of how to teach terms, facts, concepts, principles and procedures for mastery. The volume also contains some ideas on how to teach for knowledge, comprehension, application, and more complex intellectual operations.

Chapter 4
Implementing Your Mastery Learning Strategy

You have now designed your mastery learning strategy. But so far it exists only on paper. It still needs to be translated into your actual classroom teaching situation. This chapter will focus, then, on implementing the strategy in your classroom.

We have found a five-step implementation procedure to be useful.

1. Orient students to your mastery learning strategy.
2. Teach each teaching–learning unit for mastery.
3. Grade for mastery the overall learning of each of your students.
4. Report the meaning of this grade to each student.
5. Check the overall effectiveness of your program.

Orienting Students

Learning for mastery is likely to be a novel experience for your students. Accordingly, it will be helpful if you reserve some classroom time at the outset so as to orient them to your mastery learning strategy.

One phase of the orientation period should focus on *what* the students will be expected to learn for mastery, i.e., on your instructional objectives. As a general introduction to your objectives you might post and explain your course table of specifications. For a more specific statement, you might also give a different version of your final examination as a pretest. This version would test for precisely the same objectives as your final examination, but it would employ different items. These items might be drawn from those that were developed for, but not used in, constructing your final examination. They might also be constructed from scratch using the final examination items as models. For example, you might reword the final's items, taking care that your rewording does not change the meaning of the items.

A second phase of the orientation period should familiarize your students with *how* they are going to learn for mastery. Here you would concentrate on informing them about the various features of your strategy. In our own work, we have stressed the following:

1. The students are going to learn by a new method of instruction designed to help all of them learn well rather than just a few.
2. Each student will be graded *solely* on the basis of his performance on the final examination(s).
3. Each student will be graded against a predetermined performance standard and not in relation to the performance of his classmates. Indicate the standard of "A" work.
4. Each student who attains this standard will receive an "A".
5. There will be no fixed number of "A"s. Accordingly, cooperation with classmates in learning need not hurt a student's chances of earning an "A". If a student and his classmates cooperate, and all of them learn well, then all will earn "A"s.
6. Each student will receive all the help he needs so as to learn. So if a student cannot learn in one way, then alternative ways will be readily available.
7. Throughout the course, each student will be given a series of ungraded diagnostic-progress tests to promote and pace his learning. He should use the information provided by these tests to locate misunderstandings and errors in learning.
8. Each student with learning problems will be given a number of alternative learning procedures or correctives to help him overcome his particular errors and misunderstandings.
9. The student should use his choice of the suggested correctives to "correct" these errors and misunderstandings before they accumulate and impair his subsequent learning.

Teaching the Units for Mastery

Once this orientation period has been completed, begin teaching. Teach the teaching–learning units in an order which is consistent with the organization of the textbook following this cycle for each unit:

1. Present the objectives.
2. Present the group-based instructional plan.
3. Present the group-based instruction.
4. Administer the diagnostic-progress test.
5. Identify satisfactory/unsatisfactory progress in student learning.
6. Certify those students whose test performance is satisfactory.
7. "Correct" those students whose performance is not satisfactory.

8. Monitor the effectiveness of the correction phase.
9. Certify those students whose performance is now satisfactory.

The cycle may feel a bit choppy and unnatural to start, i.e., as if you are "spoon-feeding" your students. It should feel smoother and more natural later.

Presenting the Unit's Objectives

Begin by presenting your class with specific information about what they are to learn in the unit. This presentation can take one or more of several forms. You can give your students the unit table of specifications. You can pose unit study or adjunct questions (Frase, 1970; Rothkopf, 1970). Or you can provide an overview of the unit using "advance organizers" (Ausubel, 1968).

If you decide to present the unit table of specifications, then we would suggest that at least on the first unit you explain to your students what these tables mean. We would also suggest that you show them how they might use the tables to guide their study of the relevant portions of the textbook. Emphasize how the tables can be used to identify the most important content in the textbook and also the types of intellectual operations students will be expected to exhibit with each element of this content.

Should you decide to use study questions, then draw up a list of questions over the reading assignment for the unit. These questions should (a) highlight the important content present in the assignment, and (b) indicate what the student should be able to do intellectually with this content—know it, comprehend it, apply it, etc. Give this list to your students together with the assignment.

Your list can be designed in several ways. One way is to write questions which apply to the entire reading assignment. A second way is to write questions which apply to particular pages in the assignment. Each question or set of questions would be introduced with a variation of this direction: "The following question (or questions) refer to pages ___ through ___ of the reading assignment." This way of listing study questions is especially useful when the reading assignment is very lengthy, when the students are quite young, or when the students possess short spans of attention. It provides natural breaks in the reading assignment which may help the learner to better organize the material he is studying.

And if you decide to use "advance organizers," then these organizers should serve to put the unit's material into a meaningful context by relating it to the material in the previous units and to the whole course. There are three types of "organizers" we have found to be useful.

One type might be a "general topic sheet" which can be distributed to the students or written on the blackboard before the unit is presented. This sheet would typically provide the major principles and procedures which tie together the unit's material. Another type of organizer might be a "concept" or "idea" sheet. You would simply list the major concepts or ideas which are to be learned from the unit. A third type might be ongoing summaries. In a manner similar to that used in old radio serials, you could present your students with a summary or synopsis of the previous unit's material. This will help them fit the new material they are learning with the material they have already experienced.

Presenting the Unit's Group-Based Plan on Instruction

Once you have informed your students of *what* they will be expected to learn in the unit, next indicate *how* they will be expected to learn during the group-based instruction. That is, tell how you plan to teach them as a group. Such information will prove useful to your students in two regards.

On the one hand, it will avoid needless confusions in their learning. If they are given a clear idea about the basic mode or modes by which you will teach, they can pay more attention to the material presented in those modes than to the material presented in other modes. For example, if you told them you planned to lecture, it would alert them to pay more attention to what you say than to what the textbook says about particular points.

On the other, it would give your students some idea of the study strategies they might use to complement your group-based teaching method or methods. These strategies might be very simple such as note-taking, outlining, or summarizing. Or they might be more complex such as various memorization, categorization and hypothesis testing schemes. If you planned to hold a discussion, for example, then the student could plan on taking notes. Or if you planned on showing a movie, then he could plan on remembering particular points to write down once the classroom lights are turned back on. Whether simple or complex, the point is that such study strategies might give your students an advantage in processing the information you hope to present. They would help him to search for the relevant information presented and, hopefully, to gather, to organize, and to store it for future use.

Presenting the Unit's Group-Based Instruction

Begin teaching the unit. Teach it as you had planned, but do not be afraid to allow the day-to-day exigencies of classroom life to detour you from the plan if necessary. If your unit plan is sound, you will always be able to return to it.

We would encourage you to keep two things in mind as you teach. One is that your students will profit from periodic reminders of where they have been and where they are going. Thus, you may wish to call their attention to objectives already covered on the unit table of specifications and to those yet to be covered. Or you may wish to indicate the study questions they have already answered and those that remain to be answered. Or you might have them check off what they have and have not covered on their "topic-sentence" or "concept" sheets. Or you could provide brief summaries of where they have been and where they still must go.

The other thing to keep in mind is that your students will profit from being kept *actively involved with the material to be learned.* So you may wish to use some classroom techniques that will enable you to better manage student learning. We would recommend three very different management techniques.

One technique is to encourage learning throughout the lesson. A kind of encouragement we would recommend is appropriate group and individual praise for a job well-done. This is a "social" type of incentive (see p. 42).

Praise can be given orally by you (e.g., "I am really proud of you!" "This is really excellent work!"). Or it might be given by fellow students (e.g., "Let's all give Corinne a hand for her fine report!"). Praise can also be given in writing. Positive appropriate words on the student's homework, seatwork, etc., can be especially useful. Ellis B. Page (1958), for example, used the following comments: Excellent, keep it up (for the equivalent of "A" work); Good work, Keep it up (for "B" work); Perhaps try to do still better (for "C" work); Let's bring this up (for "D" work); and Let's raise this grade (for "F" work).

Another kind of encouragement we would recommend is to play on your students likes, interests, concerns. This is what we called earlier a "learner preferred activity" incentive (see page 42). Simply find out what your students like to do. Determine which of these activities you can reasonably allow. Then say, "If you will learn this unit for mastery, then you can do whichever of these activities you like."

A second classroom management technique for maintaining student involvement in learning is to use a *min-max principle* in presenting the unit's material (Trabasso, 1968). Attempt to *minimize* the salience of potentially distracting and irrelevant material. Simultaneously, attempt to *maximize* the salience of the relevant material. This may be accomplished by eliminating any materials from your classroom which might compete for your students' attention and by making the materials of interest vivid and attention-grabbing.

Suppose, for example, that you are writing some notes on the blackboard. The min-max principle would suggest you erase extraneous chalk marks and words before writing these notes. Further, it would suggest that you use chalk of different colors to highlight key points in the notes, or to print these points in, say, capital letters.

Or, to take another example, suppose you are giving a lecture. The min-max principle would suggest that you cut out asides, tangents, etc., and home in on the "meat" of your presentation. It would also suggest that you present this "meat" as vividly as possible, perhaps by a change in voice or gesticulation or by indicating that "... the following material is really important." The senior author can remember one teacher, for example, whose lectures were very attention-grabbing primarily because he outlined his main points on the blackboard before hand, referred to this outline constantly, and always summed up. Apparently this teacher had stumbled onto a key rule of thumb in public speaking: tell your audience what you're going to tell them, then tell them, and lastly tell them what you just told them.

A third technique for keeping students actively involved in learning is to use some of the classroom management techniques suggested by the work of Jacob S. Kounin (1970). Four of these techniques have been useful during a *recitation* period.[1]

1. "With-it-ness": Attempt to communicate by your behavior that you know what is going on in the classroom at all times, i.e., try to make your students feel as if you had "eyes in the back of your head." Kounin's work suggests that you stop the misbehavior of the right student or the right group of students, overlook minor misbehavior to stop major misbehavior, and stop misbehavior before it becomes serious and spreads.
2. Smoothness: Attempt to maintain the flow of the classroom activities, especially at points of transition from one activity to another. Kounin's work suggests that you try not to start an activity and leave it "hanging in midair," even if you plan to return to the activity later. It also suggests that you try to stick to the main point of an activity once it is underway, and avoid interrupting the activity for any reason not apparent to your students.
3. Momentum: Attempt to avoid behaviors that slow down the pace of the lesson. Kounin's work suggests, in particular, that you not overdwell on student behavior, on a particular point or issue, on the props used to teach (e.g., pencils, papers, books, crayons), or on directions and explanations. Also try to avoid breaking an activity into sub-parts when the activity can be performed as a single unit, or dealing with pupils one at a time when they might just as well be dealt with as part of the group.
4. Group Alerting: Attempt to keep non-participating students alert while another child is reciting or before you select a new reciter. Kounin's work suggests that you use any method to create "suspense" before calling on a child to recite: pick reciters at random so that no one knows when he will be called on; call on different children frequently; occasionally ask for whole class responses; and alert nonreciters that they might be called on in connection with what a reciter is doing or saying.

---

[1]If you are interested in acquiring some of the techniques which we describe in the following paragraphs, you can obtain self-instructional materials by writing to: Protocol Materials Development Program; Walter G. Borg, Project Director; Utah State University; Logan, Utah. These materials can either be purchased or rented for a nominal fee.

His work also suggests that you try to avoid becoming completely immersed in the performance of the reciter to the exclusion of the group, and avoid directing subsequent questions to a single new reciter without taking the group into account.

We would add that you might reseat chronic non-participants in a place in the classroom where you are likely to search for volunteers. Typically, this means reseating them in the row right in front of your desk or at the front of one of the other rows (Brophy and Good, 1974).

Kounin's fifth classroom management technique has been useful during a *seatwork* situation.

5. Variety: Attempt to avoid having the student do the same thing over and over at his seat. Kounin's work suggests that you might vary: the content of the seatwork; the type and level of intellectual operation or challenge required by the learning activity; your pattern of behavior during the session (e.g., from circulating around the class to quietly watching and observing); your instructional props; the classroom configuration (e.g., from total group to small sub-group); the child's responsibility for setting the pace or the movement of the seatwork (e.g., from being passive, to reading aloud with classmates, to pacing the learning of one other classmate); the overt behavior demanded of the child (e.g., from sedentary to vigorous); and the location of the seatwork (e.g., from the student's own desk, to another location in the classroom to outside-of-class.)

Administering the Unit Diagnostic-Progress Test

Once you have completed teaching the unit, administer the diagnostic-progress test; do *not* move on to the next unit. It might be well to alert students a couple of days in advance regarding when they will be tested. You might also remind them they will not be graded on the test. Reiterate that the test results will simply be used to inform them of their learning progress and to help improve their learning should improvement be required.

Have each student score his own test—correct/incorrect or right/wrong only—and have him score both sides of the answer sheet. You may give each student an answer key to use as he finishes, or you may read the correct answers to your class as a whole. Then collect one half of each student's corrected answer sheet.

Identifying Satisfactory/Unsatisfactory Progress in Learning

Now use their test results so as to identify students whose diagnostic progress test performance is satisfactory and students whose performance is not. An easy way to accomplish this task is to write on the blackboard the number (or the percentage) of items the student should have answered correctly if his learning is proceeding smoothly. In our own work, we have asked students to answer correctly 80% to 90% of the items on their diagnostic-progress tests.

Next, say something to the effect that "If you answered this number (or proportion) of items correctly, then your learning is proceeding smoothly. Keep it up and you are likely to earn an "A". But if you did not, then your learning is not proceeding as smoothly as it could. Let's see what we can do to get your learning back on track."

Certifying Satisfactory Progress in Learning

Ask those students whose test performance was indicative of satisfactory progress in learning to hold up their hands. Publicly congratulate them, singling out for special praise those individuals whose diagnostic-test performance has heretofore been unsatisfactory. Then ask these students to busy themselves until the next unit begins.

We have found some of these students willing and eager to serve as tutors for classmates whose diagnostic-progress test performance was unsatisfactory. So we give them a chance to use their spare time for learning how to tutor. We provide enrichment materials for the remainder of these students or allow them to engage in activities of which they are fond. The enrichment materials encourage the students to explore even further the material they have just covered.

Correcting Unsatisfactory Progress Learning

Now, gather around you the students whose test performance was indicative of unsatisfactory progress (i.e., the "correction group") and begin correction. At least for the first few units we would suggest that you use classtime for correcting. Then as students become accustomed to correcting their learning problems, you may consider asking them to use out-of-class time.

Take each diagnostic-progress test item and ask for "a show of hands" from those students who missed it. If a majority of the correction group students indicate that they have missed a particular item consider this to be indicative of a "group" learning problem. Typically, you will find that you have not adequately covered the material tested by this item in your group-based instruction. So rather than having each student review this material individually, which would be inefficient, reteach it to the whole correction group using a "reteaching" corrective. Continue using reteaching correctives until the material associated with each missed item indicative of a group-learning error has been adequately retaught.

Ostensibly the remaining test items missed by each correction group student indicate "individual" learning problems. The material covered by these items seems to have been taught thoroughly enough so that most of the class learned it. So now give each correction group student a copy of the list of correctives you prepared in Chapter 3 (minus, of course, the reteaching correctives). Explain the purpose of this list, demonstrate how to use it to pick correctives, and indicate how to use each corrective listed. This will help ensure that the student will pick correctives that are best suited to his learning requirements rather than only ones with which he is familiar.

Then have each student pick one or more correctives for restudying the material tested by *each* of the remaining diagnostic-progress test items he has missed. Put together students who choose to use "group" correctives, and bring together each student who chooses to be tutored with an appropriate tutor or turors. Next, suggest that each student use the corrective he has selected to restudy the material tested by his remaining, missed diagnostic-progress test items *in the order* that the items were missed. Because of the way you assembled your unit test (see page 31), this procedure will help ensure that the student covers individual learning problems associated with one cluster of content elements before attempting problems associated with another cluster. It will also help constrain the student to overcome the simpler learning problems associated with each cluster before attempting the harder problems.

Lastly, indicate to the whole correction group when the group-based instruction for the next unit will begin. Then give each student responsibility for using his chosen correctives beforehand to get his learning progress back on track.

Monitoring the Correction Phase

As each of your students finishes his correction, monitor how effective your correctives have been. You can do the monitoring yourself or use other students as monitors.

First, ask the finishing student what particular correctives he has used and how effective he found each one. Keep a record of his answers. Then retest the student over the unit material with which he had learning problems. For this purpose, return to the stack of 3 X 5 index cards which contains the "back-up" items for the unit. Select the back-up item for each item the student had missed on the unit diagnostic-progress test. Then administer the cards on which these items appear to the student as if they were flash cards.

Record the student's performance for each item, i.e., each card, as follows on a separate sheet of paper. First, indicate the number of the diagnostic test item to which the back-up item corresponds. Then, if the student answers the back-up item correctly, circle the number. If he answers it incorrectly, leave the number uncircled. Suppose, for example, that you administered the student the back-up item for the third item on the diagnostic-progress test. You would write ③ if the student answered the back-up item correctly or 3 if he answered it incorrectly.

Now, if the student's performance on the back-up items indicates that his unit learning progress is back to par, then praise him privately. Also make a mental note to praise the student more publicly at the outset of the next unit's group-based instruction. This procedure will help to cement in your class's mind that satisfactory learning is satisfactory learning and that it must be recognized as such, regardless of when it is attained.

Grading for Mastery

Once you have taught each unit for mastery, administer your final examination(s). It would be well to inform your students ahead of time as to when the final examination(s) will be administered.

Have students exchange answer sheets for correction and ask that the correction be done in ink. Have your students place a "X" through each incorrect answer and a circle around each correct one. Then once the last item has been corrected, have the answer sheets returned to their owner. Do not allow any students to tally the number of correct and incorrect answers on the sheet they have corrected.

Now without knowing how well any student performed on the test, once again post, or otherwise indicate, your pre-set mastery standard of "A" work. Show students how to grade their test according to this standard and let them grade themselves. This public approach to grading will help reassure them that you are not changing your standards of "A" work. It will also reinforce the idea that the "A" grade is based solely on their performance; hence, if they received an "A," then they earned it.

Hopefully the performance of most of your students will be indicative of mastery and most students will receive "A"s. If the performance of some students is not indicative of mastery, then we believe you should give no grade at all or a grade of incomplete. If you cannot do this, set out some non-mastery performance standards which are indicative of "B" work, "C" work, "D" work and "F" work. Then ask students who have not attained the mastery standard to grade themselves against these standards accordingly

Lastly, ask all students to turn in their answer sheets and their grades.

Reporting to the Student

The fourth step in implementing your mastery strategy is to report back to each student what his grade really represents. We would suggest that you give each student a modified version of your course table of specifications. In this version designate what objectives the student actually obtained and what objectives the student actually obtained and what objectives he failed to have obtained. Replace each small x in the table with the letter M when you believe the student's performance was indicative of mastery on the item or items which tested for that objective. Use the letters N/M when you believe it was not. We would also recommend that you use the letter N/M when you cannot decide whether the student's performance was indicative of mastery. Table 4-1 gives an example of such a table.

The student can then use this modified table to see how he has changed in his learning over the course of the instruction; he can see at a glance which course objectives he mastered and which ones he did not. He can also use the table to see how his grade mirrors these changes. Further, you can copy this table and place it in the student's progress file for future reference—your own or another teacher's. We are amazed to find how useful these modified tables of specifications have been in guiding future instruction for particular students.

Checking on Overall Effectiveness

The final step in implementing your mastery learning program is to check on its overall effectiveness. Clearly, if your mastery program has produced no greater student learning than your customary group-based methods, then you may want to stop teaching for mastery. But if it has produced noticeably greater student learning then you may want to continue teaching for mastery and to upgrade your program so that it produces even better results in the future.

We have found two strategies useful for judging the effectiveness of a mastery learning strategy. One assumes that you have already taught by non-mastery methods the subject that you just now taught for mastery. The other does not make this assumption.

To use the first procedure, simply calculate the percentage of students in your class who earned "A"s when the subject was taught by mastery methods and the percentage of students in your other classes who performed as well as these "A" students when the same subject was taught by non-mastery methods. If both your mastery learning class and your comparison classes took the same final examination, this second step should be a cinch. You need only determine the percentage of students in the non-mastery classes who scored as well on the final examination as the "A" students in the

Table 4-1. A Modified Course Table of Specifications

<----- Possible Operations ----->

Content	Know	Comprehend	Apply	Analyze	Synthesize	Evaluate
1. Historical Development	M					
2. Nature & Structure of Science	M					
3. Nature of Scientific Inquiry	M					
4. Biographies of Sceintists	M					
5. Measurement	M	M				
6. Chemical Materials	M	M	M			
7. Chemical Elements	M	M	N/M	N/M		
8. Chemical Change	M	M	M			
9. Chemical Laws	M	M	M	N/M		
10. Energy and Equilibrium	M	M		M		
11. Electrochemistry	M	M	M			
12. Atomic & Molecular Structure	M	M	N/M	N/M		
13. Introductory Organic Chemistry	M	M				
14. Chemistry of Life Processes	M					
15. Nuclear Chemistry	N/M	N/M	N/M			
16. Heat & Kinetic Theory	M	N/M	N/M	N/M		
17. Static/Current Electricity	M	M				
18. Magneticism/Electromagneticism	M		M			
19. Theoretical Physics	M	M	M	M		

<----- Content ----->

56

mastery class. But if your mastery learning class and your comparison classes took different final examinations, then this will be more difficult. You will have to "guestimate" what percentage of students in the non-mastery classes would have scored as well on your course final examination as did the "A" students in the mastery class. Lastly, compare the percentage of students who earned "A"s when the subject was taught by mastery methods to the percentage of students who performed as well as these "A" students when the subject was taught by non-mastery methods. If the former percentage is roughly twice as large as the latter, then you may conclude with some certainty that your mastery program has been more effective in terms of promoting student learning than your customary group-based approach to the subject.

To use the second procedure, we suggest that you use your own judgment to estimate the hypothetical percentage of students in your class you would expect to earn "A"s if your mastery program was effective. Then simply calculate the percentage of your students who did actually earn "A"s and compare this figure against the hypothetical percentage expected.

Mastery learning theory suggests that up to 95% of your students should to able to earn "A"s. But this figure has rarely been reached on a first attempt at teaching for mastery. More commonly, we find that most successful mastery learning strategies help about 30% to 50% of their students to earn "A"s the first time they are used. So, perhaps you might expect somewhere from 30% to 50% of your students to earn "A"s the first time you teach for mastery. Then each time you teach the subject for mastery again you might successively raise your expectations until they approach the 95% limit.

References

Ausubel, D. P.: *Educational Psychology: A Cognitive View*. New York: Holt, Rinehart and Winston, 1968.

Brophy, J. E., and Good, T. L.: *Teacher-Student Relationships: Causes and Consequences.* New York: Holt, Rinehart and Winston, Inc., 1974.

Frase, L. T.: "Boundary Conditions for Mathemagenic Behaviors," *Review of Educational Research, 40* (1970), 337–347.

Kounin, J. S.: *Discipline and Group-Management in Classrooms.* New York: Holt, Rinehart and Winston, Inc., 1970.

Page, E. B.: "Teacher Comments and Student Performance: A Seventy-Four Classroom Experiment in School Motivation," *Journal of Educational Psychology, 49* (1958), 173–181.

Rothkopf, E. Z.: "The Concept of Mathemagenic Activities," *Review of Education Research, 40* (1970), 325–336.

Trabasso, T.: "Pay Attention," *Psychology Today, 2* (October, 1968), 30-36.

Suggested References

Brophy, J. E. and Good, T. L.: *Teacher-Student Relationships: Causes and Consequences.* New York: Holt, Rinehart and Winston, Inc., 1974.

> This volume reviews in depth the growing body of classroom observational research. It indicates teacher behaviors that have been observed to increase student learning in the classroom. And it indicates how these behaviors might be organized so as to teach both students for whom the teacher holds high learning expectations and students for whom the teacher would typically hold low expectations. Teaching for mastery requires that the teacher hold high learning expectations for all students, especially those for whom he would typically hold low expectations.

Dunkin, M. J. and Biddle, B. J.: *The Study of Teaching.* New York: Holt, Rinehart, and Winston, 1974.

> This is a highly readable and irreverent evaluation of teaching research. On the one hand, the volume shoots down myth after myth about what a teacher should be doing in his classroom to help his students learn. On the other hand, it singles out some key teacher behaviors which do seem to result in increased student learning.

Millman, J.: "Reporting Student Progress: A Case for a Criterion-Referenced Marking System," *Evaluation and Measurement Newsletter,* No. 10 (January, 1971). (Available from the Department of Measurement and Evaluation, The Ontario Institute for Studies in Education, Toronto, Canada.

> The type of grading system we have proposed here is technically called a "criterion-referenced" or "objectives-based" grading or marking system. In this very brief paper, Millman makes a case for the use of such a grading system for the reporting of a student's school progress to the student and his parents.

Chapter 5
Some Frequently Asked Questions

As we have presented the material in Chapters 1–4 to teachers around the country, we have frequently been asked certain practical questions. In this closing chapter, we would like to share some of these questions and to indicate our answers to them. We will begin with some general questions pertaining to the material in Chapter 1 and will follow with more specific questions bearing on the material in Chapters 2, 3, and 4.

Chapter 1

Q. *Doesn't your mastery learning approach ignore many of the realities of classroom teaching?*

A. No doubt it does ignore some realities. But we believe that it does not ignore the more important of them. In particular our approach to teaching attempts to recognize that a teacher faces pressure to get through a fixed curriculum in a fixed period of time; to recognize that the bulk of this curriculum is contained in prescribed textbooks; to respect the teacher's autonomy to decide what goes on in his classroom; to appreciate the fact that most teachers already possess some successful teaching techniques; to recognize the necessarily group-based nature of classroom instruction; to recognize that different learners may have different learning requirements; and to be sensitive to the teacher's need to give grades and his students' needs to receive them.

Q. *Won't teaching for mastery require more work than my traditional approach to group-based instruction?*

A. Yes. As you might expect, the workload will be heaviest the first time you teach for mastery; it will become lighter with experience.

Q. *Then why should I teach for mastery?*

A. Two reasons. First the additional workload is not prohibitive, and the work itself is highly challenging. Second, the workload has some definite payoffs for both you and your students when completed.

For you, teaching for mastery can provide some meaningful personal rewards. Perhaps the most powerful of these is the chance to see your teaching paying off in terms of the learning of most of your students rather than just a few. Mastery learning teachers relate that they see many of their students really "turn on" to learning for the first time. The students become actively involved in learning, experience success and then ask to learn more.

For your students, teaching for mastery can increase their chances for both short-term and long-term *social survival*. On the one hand, your students will acquire some basic intellectual competencies. These competencies may help to ensure that they "can" undertake the subsequent learning demanded of them by the school and eventually by their careers. On the other, they will acquire some positive feelings toward learning. These feelings may help to ensure that they "want" to undertake this subsequent learning.

Q. *Can you give me an estimate of how much extra work teaching for mastery might require?*

A. No. It depends on too many variables—e.g., subject matter, curriculum, grade level, teacher background, social organization.

Q. *Then can you at least tell me how I might cut the extra workload that teaching for mastery might require?*

A. We have several suggestions:

1. Do not develop your mastery strategy all at once. Rather teach one piece of your course for mastery the first time. Teach an additional piece next time. Continue to teach new pieces for mastery until you can teach your whole course for mastery.

2. Develop your strategy in cooperation with one or more interested colleagues.

3. Find textbook materials which parallel your own, but which lend themselves readily to teaching for mastery. These textbooks should clearly delineate their overall instructional objectives and provide one or more examinations testing for these objectives. They should also clearly indicate the objectives of each textbook chapter or provide some sources (e.g., chapter summaries or highlights, type-set or color formats, study questions) from which these objectives might be readily inferred. Lastly, they should provide a diagnostic-progress test for each chapter. We are told that several major publishing

houses are beginning to produce curriculum materials which possess these requirements. For example, Science Research Associates has been putting together a mastery learning curriculum in modern mathematics for grades 1–8 and curriculum modules for teaching selected topics in reading and mathematics. So you might have your school librarian write some of the major textbook publishers and inquire whether they have some materials which lend themselves to teaching for mastery.

4. Borrow and then modify an existing teacher-made mastery learning strategy for your subject. Perhaps the best way to do this is to locate an existing mastery learning project and look at the materials they have developed. We would suggest that you contact the relevant government clearing houses listed on page 65 and request them to search their files for mastery learning projects related to your area. We would also suggest you try the following projects or persons.

Projects

1. "Project Mastery Learning: More Effective Instruction in Basic Skills," Nicholas Hutlock, Director, Lorain Public Schools, 3361 Garfield Boulevard, Lorain, Ohio 44052.
2. "Mastery Learning Project," Dick Phillips, Director, North Clackamas County Unified School District, 444 Lake Road, Milwaukee, Oregon 97222.
3. "Individual Mastery Learning Instructional Systems," M. Linda Eller, Director, Fremont Unified School District, 40775 Fremont Blvd., Fremont, California, 94538.
4. "The Multi-grouped Non-graded Instructional Program," C. Pate, Director, Edison Junior High School, Houston, Texas.
5. "Mastery Learning Project," Emmett Jones, Director, Olive Harvey Junior College, Chicago Junior Colleges System, Chicago, Illinois.
6. "Diagnostic Prescriptive Teaching Project," San Diego City Schools, San Diego, California.
7. "Continuous Progress Mastery," Dr. Loraine Sullivan, Director, Chicago Public Schools, Chicago, Illinois.
8. "Wingert School Project: Detroit Public Schools," Ruth Harrell, Director, Detroit Public Schools, In Service Education Program, Detroit, Michigan.
9. "Mastery Learning Project," John Telzrow, Director, Oberlin City Schools, Oberlin, Ohio 44074.

People

1. Lorin W. Anderson
   School of Education
   University of South Carolina
   Columbia, South Carolina
2. James H. Block
   Department of Education
   Unviersity of California
   Santa Barbara, California
3. Benjamin S. Bloom
   Department of Education
   University of Chicago
   Chicago, Illinois
4. Mildered E. Kersh
   School of Education
   University of Washington
   Seattle, Washington

5. J. W. Moore
   School of Education
   Bucknell University
   Lewisburg, Pennsylvania
6. James R. Okey
   School of Education
   Indiana University
   Bloomington, Indiana
7. Samuel N. Postlethwait
   Department of Biological
      Sciences
   Purdue University
   West Lafayette, Indiana 47907
8. J. G. Sherman
   Department of Psychology
   Georgetown University
   Washington, D.C.

5. Adopt an existing, commercial mastery learning strategy or a commercial individualized teaching strategy that might readily be converted into a learning for mastery strategy. Gronlund's volume *Individualizing Classroom Instruction* (New York: MacMillan Publishing Co., 1974) provides a good summary of the commercial strategies available, as well as addresses for obtaining them.

Q. *What will teaching for mastery mean for my role as a teacher?*

A. We see your role as that of a craftsman who is concerned with the management of individual learning within a group context. You are a *craftsman* in the sense that your teaching will reflect elements of both a science and an art. Like a science, your craft will enable you to produce basically the same result time after time, viz, increased learning for most students. But like an art, it will enable you to utilize your own personal touches in producing these results. You will essentially decide what learning will be increased and how it will be increased.

We see you executing the following managerial activities in practicing your craft in the classroom.

1. *Valuing*. You will make explicit value judgments about what your students are to learn and to what standard.
2. *Planning*. You will design the instructional "blueprint" under which all of your students will learn for mastery.

3. *Assembling.* You will assemble the materials called for by your blueprint.

4. *Quality controlling.* You will see that these materials are used according to your blueprint.

5. *Evaluating.* You will determine the extent to which your instructional "blueprint" actually helped your students to learn what you wanted them to learn for mastery.

Q. *Can I really learn this role?*

A. Yes. Any craft can be learned. But it takes patience, practice and constant tinkering with basic techniques.

Q. *What will teaching for mastery mean for my students' role as learners?*

A. We believe that it will encourage more of your students to accept personal responsibility for their learning, since the grade one receives is the grade he has earned. The student cannot say he earned a low grade only because he didn't perform as well as his classmates. Nor can he say that he earned a low grade because he was not given the help he needed to learn. All he can say is that his learning was not up to standard.

Chapter 2

General

Q. *Doesn't your approach to mastery learning put much faith in my judgment and intuition? After all, who am I to define mastery for students?*

A. Yes. We do so because we assume that you are a teaching professional. Such professionals know their subject matter, i.e., *what* they teach, and *how* to teach it. They are also empathic to the needs of their students and sensitive to the demands of the school. If teaching professionals cannot be trusted to exercise their good judgment and intuition in defining mastery for their students, then who can be trusted?

Q. *Isn't there more to the idea of mastery than performing to a particular standard on a final examination?*

A. Yes. There are also the positive self-sentiments of pride and satisfaction, what White (1959) called "feelings of efficacy," that go along with performing to this standard. These self-sentiments derive directly from the fact that the student's performance to standard on the final reflects his ability to meet a particular challenge posed by his learning environment. He was asked to acquire a particular set of intellectual competencies (i.e., objectives) and he did in fact interact effectively with his learning environment to acquire them.

It is our belief that if we can provide students with certain intellectual competencies in one small part of their learning environment and, hence, the associated feelings of efficacy, then perhaps both these competencies and feelings might generalize to other parts of this environment. If so, they might encourage the student to take up the intellectual challenges posed in these parts.

On Selecting Instructional Objectives

Q. Aren't some school subjects better candidates for mastery learning than others?

A. No. We believe that it is possible to define instructional objectives which all students are expected to master in each school subject.

Q. Isn't it easier to define instructional objectives in some subjects than in others?

A. Yes. We have found it easiest to define objectives in subjects that tend to be *closed* rather than open, and to emphasize *convergent* rather than divergent thinking. We are speaking here of basic subjects such as reading and arithmetic, of introductory subjects such as first year English and Algebra, and of structured subjects such as mathematics, science, and history. Closed subjects are composed of a finite set of ideas and possible intellectual operations with those ideas. They are also subjects whose basic content has not changed nor is likely to change radically for some time (Bloom, 1971). Convergent subjects are those in which students are expected to obtain appropriate answers or solutions to problems through customary problem modes (Guilford, 1959).

We would reemphasize one point, however. Just because it is easier to define instructional objectives in some subjects than others, it does not follow that these other subjects cannot be taught for mastery. We reiterate *any* school subject can be taught for mastery.

Q. Can my course objectives by physical (Harrow, 1972), emotional (Krath-wohl et al., 1964), and/or interpersonal (Menges and McGaghie, 1974) as well as intellectual?

A. Yes. We see no reason why you cannot teach certain physical, emotional, or interpersonal skills for mastery. You would only have to modify appropriately the procedures presented here.

Q. *Suppose the Bloom, Hastings and Madaus (1971) volume does not cover the area I wish to teach for mastery or covers it poorly. Where might I then obtain some idea of worthy instructional objectives for my subject?*

A. You might write to one or more of the following government clearing houses. Request documents indicating what objectives subject matter experts feel you might cover and ask to receive their newsletters.

Career Education, 204 Gurler, Northern Illinois University, 60115. Dr. David Tiedeman, Director.

The Disadvantaged, Teachers College, Box 40, Columbia University, New York, N.Y. 10027. Dr. Edmund W. Gordon, Director.

Early Childhood Education, University of Illinois, 805 W. Pennsylvania, Urbana, Illinois 61801. Dr. Lilian G. Katz, Director.

Handicapped and Gifted. The Council for Exceptional Children, 1411 South Jefferson Davis Highway, Jefferson Plaza #1, Suite 900, Arlington, Va. 22202. Dr. Donald Erickson, Director.

Languages and Linguistics, Modern Language Association of America, 62 Fifth Avenue, New York, N.Y. 10011. Mr. Warren C. Born, Director.

Reading and Communication Skills, 1111 Kenyon Road, Urbana, Illinois 61801. Dr. Bernard O'Donnell, Director.

Rural Education and Small Schools, New Mexico State University, Box 3AP, Las Cruces, New Mexico 88003. Dr. Everett Edington, Director.

Science, Mathematics and Environmental Education, Ohio State University, 1800 Cannon Drive, 400 Lincoln Tower, Columbus, Ohio 43221. Dr. Robert W. Howe, Director.

Social Studies/Social Science Education, 855 Broadway, Boulder, Colorado 80302. Dr. Robert Fox, Director.

On Constructing the Final Examination

Q. *Need I construct a final examination at all? Why not test for mastery as I go along?*

A. Some mastery strategies tend not to use a final examination (see Block, 1974). Rather, they test for the course objectives as the student encounters them in various segments of the course.

Our reason for using a final examination is simple. We believe that mastery over *each segment* of a course is not the same as mastery over the *whole* course. The final examination taps mastery over the whole course.

Q. *Can I construct my final examination during the course rather than before it begins?*

A. We would recommend against this procedure since constructing the final examination beforehand can be so valuable. First, it may help you to clarify more precisely what it is that you really expect your students to master. As you write the test items, you may find that some of your objectives were a trifle fuzzy. Second, it gives you a relatively unambiguous way of communicating to your students what they will be expected to carry away from the course. As noted in Chapter 4, you can give the students another form of the final as a pretest. The students can then keep this form as a study guide. Third, it may help you to prepare a better final examination since you can take time to make a good test. And finally, it may save you instructional time. You need not waste precious teaching time to prepare the final examination.

There *is* one situation in which you might want to *revise* your final examination during the course. Suppose that during the course you decide to add some objectives to your course table of specifications and/or to drop others. You might then revise your final examination to reflect these changes.

Q. *Why do you recommend against the use of essay-type items on the final examination?*

A. Typically such items are hard to score for mastery/nonmastery in student learning. If you can devise some sound ways of scoring them (see Coffman, 1971 for some hints), then by all means use some essay items on your final examination.

Q. *Need I give a pencil and paper final examination?*

A. No. You may use any means you like of determining whether your students have or have not mastered your course objectives (e.g., oral exams, term papers, projects, etc.). Remember, though, that you may encounter some problems in scoring for mastery the results produced by non-paper and pencil testing instruments.

Q. *Can I use a standardized test as my final examination?*

A. Yes, if its items test for your course objectives. If only some of its items do so, then use only those particular items.

On Setting a Mastery Performance Standard

Q. *What are the characteristics of an ideal performance standard?*

A. According to Block (1972), the ideal standard

(a) would derive from the same set of values that guided your choice of instructional objectives; hence, it would not be a value free standard;

(b) would be non-arbitrarily derived in the sense that you could logically or empirically defend its superiority vis-à-vis other possible standards;

(c) would be absolute in three senses: it would separate students into two groups—the masters and the non-masters—and would not misclassify a non-master as a master or vice-versa; it would judge student learning solely on the basis of that learning and not in terms of one's learning relative to his peers; it would be the only criterion used to judge a student's learning; and

(d) would be attainable given reasonable amounts of human (teacher and student) and non-human resources and time.

Q. *Wouldn't perfect performance on the final examination be an ideal standard?*

A. No. Perfect performance does not possess characteristics *b* and *d* of ideal standard.

Q. *What if my definition of mastery proves to be poor?*

A. Revise it before you teach for mastery again. Begin by revising your course objectives. Simply go to the progress files of your students, pull the modified version of the course table of specifications you have placed in each student's file, and collate the information provided in these tables. Look for course objectives for which more than 20 to 25% of your students received *N/M*'s.

Once you have identified these objectives, decide which ones were unrealistic to expect your students to master. Drop these objectives from your course table of specifications or modify them accordingly. And revise your final examination to test for the objectives which still remain in the course table.

Now revise your mastery performance standards. For this purpose consider the diagnostic-progress and the retest results (if any) of each student on each unit. Give the student a score of 2 if his learning progress was satisfactory on the unit with or without the aid of correctives and a score of 1 if it was unsatisfactory even with the aid of the correctives.

Add up the scores for each individual across all the teaching–learning units. Call this the student's "progress consistency" score. Then rank all of your students according to their progress consistency scores. List those students with the highest scores first and those with the lowest scores last. And identify the students in the top 1/3 or the top 1/4 of the list. Ostensibly, these were the most consistent learners in the class.

Now determine how these consistent learners performed on the final examination. If you used a total test score as your mastery standard, then list the total test scores earned by your consistent learners from the highest score to the lowest. Throw out, say, the bottom two or three scores in your list and likewise the top two or three. Any of the scores that remain might be used as your new mastery standard.

If you used sub-scores or objective-by-objective scores as your mastery standard, then follow the same general procedure. List from the highest to the lowest the sub-scores or scores earned by your most consistent students for a particular content area, intellectual operation, or objective. Again throw out, say, the bottom and top two or three scores in your list. Use any of the scores that remain as your new mastery performance standard for the particular content area, intellectual operation or objective of interest. Then repeat this procedure for the sub-scores or scores earned by your most consistent students on each other content area, intellectual operation or objective.

Needless to say, you need not set any new mastery standards for those particular objectives you decided to drop from your course table of specifications. Nor need you set any new standards for a particular content area or a particular type of intellectual operation if you have decided to drop all those objectives which pertain to that area of operation.

Chapter 3

General

Q. *Is all of this planning really necessary?*

A. We believe so. Teaching for mastery requires that you be more proactive than reactive in your teaching—you are to steer the teaching-learning process rather than to be steered by it. This planning gives you an opportunity to be more proactive in your teaching. It helps you to anticipate possible instructional contingencies. Should these contingencies occur, then you are ready for them.

On Identifying Teaching–Learning Units

Q. *Need I use my textbook's chapters as teaching–learning units?*

A. No. You may break up your textbook in any way you find convenient.

Q. *Need each of my teaching–learning units cover the same amount of material?*

A. No. You may want your earlier units to cover less material than your later one. This will help to cut the amount of material students are expected to learn for mastery while they are also learning how to learn for mastery.

Q. *Can my teaching–learning units be shorter than 10 to 14 days?*

A. We would recommend that they not be shorter. If your units are shorter, then neither you nor your students may have an opportunity to piece together each unit's material into a meaningful whole. Hence this material may remain fragmented in your students' minds and easily forgotten.

Q. *Can I let my teaching–learning units run for a month or more?*

A. We would not recommend it. In this period of time, some of your students could encounter deep-seated learning problems with each unit's material that you might never be able to correct. Units of about two weeks' length allow you to catch student learning problems at a time when most of these problems are easily corrected.

On Planning the Teaching–Learning Units: The Group-Based Instruction

Q. *Need the initial presentation of a unit's material be group-based?*

A. No. In fact, many mastery learning approaches (e.g., Keller's Personalized System of Instruction and Postlethwait's Audio-Tutorial Instruction) package each teaching–learning unit's material for use by individual students. The students then go through each unit's material at their own pace. If you wish to package your teaching learning units for individual use then you might want to read James Russell's *Modular Instruction* (Minneapolis: Burgess Publishing Co., 1974).

Q. *Why, then, do you recommend using a group-based model?*

A. We have two basic reasons. First, we recognize that group-based instruction is a basic fact of life in most school situations. Rather than choosing to ignore this fact or to decry its existence, we have chosen to capitalize upon it and to ask how we might better individualize ordinary group-based instruction. Second, we do not believe that group-based approaches to instruction are as bad as their critics make them out to be. In our own work we find that they are effective and efficient ways to teach most of a unit's material to most students and that they can easily be supplemented to teach the remaining material to the remaining students. Further, we find that group-based approaches to instruction are highly *individualized* in their own way. In particular they recognize the *social* nature of individuals and attempt to teach individuals in ways which reflect this nature.

Q. *You tell me to go about planning my group-based instruction for each unit as I normally would. But later you also tell me that my group-based approach may not reach some students on some material and that I need to develop unit correctives to teach this material to these students. Why can't I strengthen my group-based instructional plan for each unit with correctives from the start?*

A. You could. The question is, which correctives would you add to your group-based plans? Until you teach each unit you really have no idea of which correctives are likely to best supplement each unit's group-based instruction.

Q. *As I read your approach to mastery learning, it's not my group-based instruction that is the key to optimizing my students' learning. It's what I do after the group-based instruction. Am I right?*

A. Yes. We view the key to optimizing student learning to be the feedback/correction procedures you use to monitor and to supplement the on-going effectiveness of your group-based instruction. If your diagnostic-progress tests tell you where students are having problems learning from your group-based instruction, and if your correctives overcome these problems, then most of your students should be able to learn well.

On Planning the Teaching–Learning Units: The Diagnostic-Progress Tests

Q. *Can't I use existing unit quizzes rather than constructing a new diagnostic-progress tests?*

A. Yes, provided that the quizzes really do tap each of the unit's objectives. Remember you need information about how each student is changing relative to each unit objective for purposes of correction.

Q. *Why can't I just test students over a sample of each unit's objectives as I would normally do?*

A. You could, if you were sure that every student would answer all of the test items for the sampled objectives correctly. But suppose some students did not. How could you tell where each student's learning problems lay? Did the student fail to learn just the particular objectives tested? Or did he also fail to learn some objectives whose attainment was prerequisite to attaining the particular objectives tested? Your test results might not be able to give you this information. Yet such information is crucial for correction purposes.

Q. *Can I use essay items on the unit tests?*

A. We would recommend against it. Essay items take much time to answer and to score. Remember you do not want the diagnostic-progress testing to take up inordinate amounts of teaching time.

Q. *Need I construct pencil and paper diagnostic-progress tests?*

A. No, as long as the non-pencil and paper tests do not take too long to complete and to score.

Q. *Need I construct "formal" diagnostic-progress tests?*

A. No. Some teachers have found a host of informal ways to give diagnostic-progress tests. They have used diagnostic-progress homework assignments, classroom exercises, questions in class, etc. We would point out, though, that these teachers began by constructing formal diagnostic-progress tests and then found informal substitutes for these tests as they gained more experience in teaching for mastery.

On Planning the Teaching-Learning Units: The Correctives

Q. *Why can't I just reteach all the problematic material revealed by the unit diagnostic-progress tests and not bother developing correctives?*

A. First, it would be inefficient. Chances are that at least a couple of students may have failed to obtain each objective in the unit. You would be forced, then, to reteach each objective in the unit. Second, reteaching would still probably be ineffective. Chances are that you would find it difficult to reteach the material in as many different ways as might be required by your students' different learning requirements. And even if you could, you and some of your students might get bored as you went over the same material in the different ways.

Q. *How many correctives should I provide?*

A. It is not the number of correctives you provide, but the *variety* that is important. To start, we suggest you develop, say, a dozen to a half a dozen correctives. Be sure that these correctives present the unit's material and/or involve the students in its learning in ways very different from each other. Then watch as the students select from this menu of correctives. Subsequently revise the menu by paring ineffective correctives and replacing them with new ones to be tested.

Q. *How might I limit the number of correctives I develop?*

A. One way is to limit the number of neglected modalities, abilities, and incentives you will choose to emphasize in your correctives. Which ones you choose to emphasize is essentially up to you. In our own experience, we have found that most teachers tend to develop correctives which emphaszie visual and tactile modalities, spatial ability, internal incentives, and learner-preferred activity external incentives.

Another way to limit the number of correctives you develop is to inventory the types of instructional materials to which you have access in your classroom and elsewhere. Your librarian, media and curriculum specialists, and colleagues can be very useful in this regard. This inventory will likely show that you simply lack the materials needed to develop certain types of correctives.

Q. *Suppose I can provide only one or two correctives. Have you any suggestions?*

A. Yes. We would suggest that you rely on the all purpose presentational/involvement correctives such as tutoring and small-group study sessions. We have been amazed, and pleased, with how well students can teach their classmates. They communicate with their classmates in ways upon which an older person might never hit, and they seem to know almost intuitively what incentives to offer for learning.

Q. *Can I tutor myself?*

A. Yes. But plan to teach the material differently than in the group-based instruction.

Q. *Isn't the use of student to teach other students a case of the "blind leading the blind?"*

A. It would be if the students were blind, in your case, if the student-teachers did not know what they were talking about. But you can guard against this possibility by being sure that each student teaches only that material which his diagnostic-progress test results indicate he is qualified to teach.

Q. *Why did you ask me to begin developing my own correctives by analyzing my group-based instructional plan rather than my students' learning requirements? Wouldn't it have been better to ask how each of my students needs to have a unit's material presented, then to ask how I plan to present it? And wouldn't it have been better to ask how each of my students needs to be involved with this material than to ask how I plan to involve them?*

A. We can give two reasons for our approach. First, most classroom teachers do not have the kinds of detailed information needed to determine a student's particular learning requirements until the instruction is underway. Such information would not prove useful in teaching a course for mastery from the outset.

Second, it is the characteristics of your group-based instructional plan which ultimately determine the student learning characteristics that will be utilized in your course. So once you know how you plan to teach your group-based instruction, you also know what kinds of student learning characteristics your plan will utilize. If your plan plays on a narrow range of characteristics (e.g., verbal ability), then you know almost automatically that only a small percentage of students will possess the resources to learn from it. Hence, you can broaden the plan through appropriate correctives so that it plays on a wider range of characteristics (e.g., verbal and non-verbal abilities). Thereby you increase the percentage of students who will possess the resources necessary to learn from your instruction.

Q. *Where should I locate the various correctives I have developed?*

A. We suggest that you put them into some type of learning or resource center. This center may be located in your classroom if you have the same students all day. It may be located elsewhere (e.g., library or study rooms) if you have different students throughout the day. This will enable your mastery learning students to make use of the center outside of the class as well as within it.

You may also want to arrange to have your center open before and after school. Students serve admirably as center monitors.

Chapter 4

On the Orientation Period

Q. *Is the orientation period really necessary?*

A. We believe that the orientation period is crucial. Think of teaching for mastery as the planting of a new seed in the classroom environment. Lest this seed die aborning, you need to carefully prepare the soil of the learning environment, i.e., your students, to receive it.

Q. *Doesn't the orientation period have a spoon-feeding flavor?*

A. Yes. But we think that this spoon-feeding is vastly preferable (at least initially) to letting students discover for themselves how to learn for mastery. Suppose that you did allow your students to go the discovery route. If some of them failed to learn well in your course, then you wouldn't know whether they were poor learners or poor discoverers. Perhaps these students might have been perfectly capable of learning if what they were supposed to have learned had been pointed out to them.

We would also point out that the spoon-feeding has seemed to stimulate rather than squash students efforts to learn how to learn for themselves (see Chapter 1). Apparently, the spoon-feeding on how to learn early in a mastery learning program may help free the student to feed himself later.

Q. *Can I administer my final examination as a pretest, rather than a version of it, so as to orient my students to my course objectives?*

A. We would recommend that you did not. The point of administering a pretest is to give your students a very specific study guide to your course objectives. You probably would not want to allow your students to use the final examination as a study guide.

Q. *During the orientation period you suggest that I indicate my standards of "A" work. If I also have standards of "B", "C", "D", and "F" work, should I indicate them at this time too?*

A. No. In our work we find that if you allow the student the option to do other than "A" work, then some students will take advantage of the option. In college and high school, for example, many persons opt to take a "gentlemen's 'C'" or the easy "B".

Q. *Doesn't this orientation procedure provoke anxiety among students who have traditionally not earned "A" grades?*

A. Yes, it does provoke some anxiety. But we try to counter this anxiety by pointing out that each student is going to be given all the help he needs to earn the "A" and that we believe that each student can really earn an "A". We also point out that there will no longer be a limited number of "A"s. So if one works hard and learns well, then his "A" is not going to be snatched away from him just because a handful of his peers happened to have learned better.

Q. *If I tell all my students that they can earn an "A", does not the "A" grade become meaningless as a motivator?*

A. Our experience suggests that giving everyone a chance to earn an "A" grade does not diminish the grade's power to motivate. In fact, we are surprised at the number of students who dismissed the importance of "A" grades until they were given a real chance to earn one.

We would point out, though, that most of our experience has been with students who have been taught for mastery once or twice. Perhaps as students are taught for mastery over longer periods of time, the grade will lose its appeal. By this time, however, we hope that students will have come to realize that what is really important in school learning is not the grade that one receives but the feelings of competence (cf. White, 1959) that arise out of knowing that one has learned certain things well. If so, the desire to feel competent, not the mark one receives, will provide all the motive that the students need for learning.

Q. *What about students who believe they are fundamentally incapable of earning an "A"?*

A. Good question. We are presently attempting to develop strategies to get through to these students. To lay out the underpinnings for these strategies would take us into academic self-concept theory and is beyond the scope of this volume. Suffice it to say, these strategies focus on circumventing the "I am a loser" syndrome by temporarily disengaging a student's actual academic performance and his academic self-concept.

On Teaching the Teaching-Learning Units: Teaching from the Textbook

Q. *What if my textbook is terribly disorganized? Do I have to follow its organization in teaching the teaching-learning units?*

A. No. We suggested that you follow the textbook's organization so that you wouldn't skip around the textbook as you teach. As we pointed out, skipping around in the teaching of your text might not be tough for you, but it could be for your students.

We have found two useful ways to reorganize disorganized textbooks that enable one to teach the textbook without skipping around too much. Both schemes pivot on rearranging the textbook's chapters, i.e., the teaching-learning units. In the first scheme, one tries to arrange the chapters so that the material in one chapter builds *directly* upon the material in the preceding chapter. We call this *linear* sequencing. In the second scheme, one tries to arrange the chapters so that the material in one chapter builds *indirectly* upon the material in one or more of the preceding chapters. We call this *hierarchical* sequencing. Both approaches help to ensure that once you teach the material in one chapter for mastery, you should not have to reteach it from scratch later.

On Teaching the Teaching-Learning Units: The Group-Based Instruction

Q. *Don't you use the group-based instruction for pacing student learning as well as for conveying each unit's material?*

A. Yes. This way of pacing student learning helps to ensure that the teacher gets through his fixed curriculum in the fixed amount of calendar time he has available for teaching. It helps all students to get off on the same foot in learning each unit's material. Thus it helps avoid a problem that occurs time and time again when students are allowed to pace their own learning—*procrastination* in beginning to learn.

Q. *Suppose my students do not possess study strategies that complement my customary group-based teaching methods?*

A. You might suggest some strategies. Books on how to study are filled with suggestions.

Q. *What if a student is absent during some portions of the group-based instruction.*

A. Treat him as you would normally treat him. Your correctives should help him to cover the material he has missed.

Q. *You talk about the management of learning. What about the management of learners (e.g., discipline and punishment)?*

A. Mastery learning is relatively unconcerned with the management of learners. It is not that we assume the management of learners is an unimportant aspect of classroom life. Clearly it is. It is that we assume (along with Sarason, 1971) that problems with the management of *learners* stem from problems with the management of *learning*. If you can better manage your students' learning, we believe that you will need to spend less time managing their behavior.

Q. *Isn't it tougher to keep some students actively involved with the material to be learned during a unit's group-based instruction than others?*

A. Yes. Younger children are especially problematic. Sometimes they will attend to a particular learning activity for long periods of time and other times they will attend to it only momentarily. Older students are also problematic. Many of them have already come to learn that school is a boring place which does not warrant their attention. It is precisely because there are individual differences among students in terms of their attentiveness that we have proposed several different strategies for keeping your students actively involved in learning rather than one. We suggest you try all three strategies.

Q. *How much active involvement can I expect?*

A. We really do not know at this point how much involvement is required for optimal learning. We would speculate, however, that you need not demand *total* involvement from your students.

Q. *Will I always be able to tell when my students are actively involved in learning?*

A. No. Our own research suggests that there are times when a student may be covertly involved with the material and yet not reflect this involvement in his overt behavior.

Q. *Is there any way I can estimate how involving my group-based instruction is?*

A. Yes. Write Lorin Anderson for an observational checklist.

Q. *Surely there is more to teaching my particular subject than you have indicated. Where might I find some general research on teaching and especially research on teaching my particular subject?*

A. See the following excellent sources:
1. Brophy, J. E. and Good, T. L. *Teacher-Student Relationships: Causes and Consequences.* New York: Holt, Rinehart and Winston, 1974.
2. Dunkin, M. J. and Biddle, B. J. *The Study of Teaching.* New York: Holt, Rinehart and Winston, 1974.
3. Gage, N. L. (ed.). *Handbook of Research on Teaching.* Chicago: Rand McNally, 1968.
4. Gagné, R. M. *Essentials of Learning for Instruction.* Hinsdale, Illinois: The Dryden Press, 1974.
5. Travers, R. M. W. (ed) *The Second Handbook of Research on Teaching.* Chicago: Rand McNally, 1973.

On Teaching The Teaching-Learning Units: Diagnostic-Progress Testing

Q. *Besides using the unit's group-based instruction to pace student learning, don't you also use the unit's diagnostic-progress testing for pacing?*

A. Yes. The periodic diagnostic-progress tests encourage students to keep up in their learning.

Q. *Don't I have to worry about cheating if the students score their own diagnostic-progress tests?*

A. No. Since the tests are ungraded, cheating cannot raise the student's grade. It also cannot erase the fact that the student's actual tests results indicated that he had not attained particular objectives.

Q. *Why not demand perfect performance on the test as a standard of satisfactory learning progress?*

A. Our work suggests that perfect performance may be unnecessary to demonstrate that a student had adequately learned a unit's material. It also indicates that demanding perfect performance may be detrimental to students' feelings about the material they are learning.

Q. *Why not grade for mastery the unit diagnostic-progress test results?*

A. Some mastery learning strategies do grade the unit test results (see Block, 1974) and award grades on the basis of the number of separate units mastered. We can give two reasons against this practice, though. First, mastery of each unit may not be synonymous with mastery of the course taken as a whole. Second, if the student fails to master several units early in the course, then he may quit trying to learn for mastery. His initial failures may preclude him from having a chance to earn an "A" no matter how well he learns in the latter part of the course.

On Teaching the Teaching–Learning Units: Correction

Q. *Doesn't the process of correction rob the better student?*

A. The correction process certainly does shift teacher attention and certain basic instructional resources away from the better students to the poorer ones. Let us ask, however, what the better students gain in return for this loss of attention and resources? First, they gain the opportunity and time to engage in enrichment or other activities. They need not sit idly by while the teacher reteaches problematic material to a handful of their classmates. Second they gain the opportunity and time to learn how to teach. The bulk of students with whom we have worked find this opportunity and time to be academically challenging and personally rewarding. Many also indicate, for the first time, some sympathy and understanding for their classmates' learning problems. Third, they eventually gain better prepared classmates. Speaking hyperbolically, the situation becomes somewhat akin to participating in a class where all students are honor students. The better student's classmates become less of a drain on his learning and more of a prod to learn even better.

Q. *How much time should I allow for correction?*

A. On the whole, you have only so much time available for correction. The combined time spent in group-based instruction and in correction across all the teaching-learning units should not exceed the calendar time you have available for teaching. We suggest, therefore, that you let each unit's diagnostic-progress test results help determine how much of this whole time to use for correction on each unit. If the test results are generally poor, then allow more time. This will typically be the case on the early units. Then as the test results improve, allow less time.

We also suggest that you allow some extra correction time at the course's outset. This will allow the students to explore the correctives available to them and to find ones that are best suited to their learning requirements. It will also give them time to become accustomed to the idea that you really do expect them to overcome their particular learning problems.

Q. *Where will I find class time for correction on the early units in my course?*

A. Borrow it from class time that you had planned to spend on teaching the later units. If your mastery strategy works as it should, then we believe that you should not need the time you have borrowed in order to teach these later units effectively.

Q. *Why can't I assign students to particular correctives? Why should students be allowed to choose their own?*

A. Two reasons. One is that the student probably knows his learning requirements far better than you—at least initially. The other is that if the student is allowed to choose his own correctives, then he may be more likely to assume personal responsibility for their use.

Q. *What if some of my students are not ready to assume personal responsibility for using their correctives?*

A. You might want to provide some initial encouragements for these students to correct their individual learning problem. Then, as they become more willing to accept personal responsibility for using their correctives, you can phase out these encouragements.

In our own work we have used as encouragements for correcting individual learning problems some of the management of learning techniques we asked you to consider in connection with your group-based instruction. You might refer back to pages 49–51 for fuller discussion of these techniques. In addition, we have used two other encouragement strategies.

First, we have encouraged each student to think of his performance like the proverbial glass that is half-full rather than half-empty. Thus, if a learner has attained a score of 13 on his diagnostic-progress and a score of 17 is indicative of satisfactory progress, then we have encouraged the student to remember that he has already earned a score of 13 and need be able to learn the material associated with only four more of the items he has missed to demonstrate satisfactory progress on the unit. We have not emphasized that he was able to answer *only* 13 items correctly.

Second, we have encouraged students to learn cooperatively with their classmates. This gives them a chance to be used by their peers as a resource person. Thus, they earn rewards for the expertise they already possess while at the same time adding to that expertise by correcting their own learning problems.

Q. *What if some students do not finish correcting their unit learning problems in the time allowed?*

A. We suggest that you retest these students shortly before the group-based instruction for the next unit begins. Encourage them to continue restudying the material which they have not yet reached and assign them to a tutor or a small study group. Then begin your group-based instruction for the new unit. This procedure will help ensure that you do not hold up the learning progress of the bulk of your class for a few students. It will also help cement in these students' minds that you expect them to stay up and that they are going to be given the individual help they need to stay up. The message these students will receive is that you are going to proceed with your instruction but you have no intention of letting their learning problems slide and of leaving them too far behind.

Q. *What good is the information I gather on each teaching–learning unit regarding the correctives my students have used?*

A. This information can give you some useful insights regarding how you might strengthen your group-based instruction for a given unit the next time you teach for mastery. You may want to build in some of the more effective correctives (e.g., the use of small groups) into your group-based plan. Or you may want to build in some of the presentational and/or involvement techniques represented by these more effective correctives.

On Grading for Mastery

Q. *Doesn't your approach place heavy emphasis on a single final examination or set of examinations?*

A. Yes it does. That is why some teachers with whom we have worked have decided on administering several final examinations during their courses. But there are problems with this approach. First, it may make the teacher divulge his standards of "B", "C", "D", and "F" work. Once such standards are known the student may opt to quit trying for an "A" and shoot for one of the other grades. Second, it may squash certain students' beliefs that they can earn "A"s. If the student's performance on an early exam is bad, it may preclude him from earning an "A" no matter how well he performs on the other exams.

Q. *Why grade at all?*

A. One practical answer is that you have no choice in the matter. But even if you do have a choice there are good reasons to continue grading.

One reason is the nature of our society. Like it or not, grades are the primary-currency of exchange for many of the goods, services, and privileges that our society has to offer individuals. Grades can be exchanged for such diverse entities as cash (when parents pay their children a dollar for each "A"), parental approval, teacher approval, peer approval privileges (e.g., the opportunity to work in the library by oneself), and the opportunity for higher education or for a good-paying job. To deprive students of grades, then, is to possibly deprive them of our society's goods, services, and privileges.

A second reason is habit. Students are used to receiving grades and they are used to teachers giving them. Some students, in fact, even equate grades with learning. To deprive students of grades, therefore, is to ask them to break a deeply ingrained habit. And, for some students, it is to face the frightening possiblity that they will have no way of knowing whether they have in fact learned.

The reader should note, however, that while we use grades, in our mastery learning strategy grades have a fundamentally different meaning than is typically the case. In the ordinary school, non-mastery learning situation, the grades one receives may be relatively uncorrelated with what he has learned in any absolute sense. This is because his grades typically depend on how well he has learned relative to his peers. Thus, he may learn very poorly indeed and still receive an "A" because his peers performed more poorly. Or the student may learn very well indeed and still receive a "C" because his peers performed even better.

But in a mastery learning situation, the grades one receives are correlated with what the student has learned in an absolute sense. Thus, if a student achieves to a particular level, he receives the grade corresponding to that level irrespective of his classmates' performance.

Grades in a mastery learning situation, therefore, reflect the students' learning alone. They do not reflect the students' learning relative to that of his peers. Put is another way, in mastery learning a student is graded for learning and not graded for with whom he learned. We believe that *grading for learning* can trigger the students' intrinsic or internal motives to learn.

Q. *Can I use pass/fail grades?*

A. We would recommend that you do not. Passing a course is not the same as mastering it. Usually a passing grade means little more than the student did just enough not to earn a failing grade.

Q. *Suppose everyone earns an "A", won't "A" grades not matter any more?*

A. As we pointed out earlier, this may well be the case. We are far less concerned that the grade itself matter than that what the grade actually represents matters. We hope that by the time students may become blasé about receiving "A" grades, they will become excited about possessing the particular intellectual competencies represented by the "A" grade.

Q. *Will any administrator tolerate a teacher who gives out too many "A"s?*

A. Probably no administrator will tolerate a teacher whose students have been *given* "A"s. But most of the administrators with whom we have dealt had no qualms about a teacher whose students have clearly *earned* many "A"s. In judging whether a teacher's students have really earned many "A"s or have simply been given them, these administrators have tended to consider two basic points. Are the teacher's standards as high as they used to be? Has the "A" students' performance really been up to these standards? If the teachers standards have not slipped and the "A" students really did perform to these standards, these administrators have accepted the teacher's grades.

Q. *Suppose most of my students earn "A"s but a few do not. Are not those few students more conspicuous failures in your mastery learning approach to instruction than they would be in a conventional non-mastery approach (Spady, 1974)?*

A. We do not know.

Q. *Suppose that none of my students attain mastery as I have defined it?*

A. This is a tough question. You are caught with the transition problem of going from a relative system of grading, in which sliding standards can be used to adjust for poor learning or teaching, to a more absolute system in which such sliding standards cannot legitimately be used.

Our first impulse is to say that standards are standards and that if the mastery standard was not attained, then none of your students should be given "A"s. But this approach assumes that the students were solely responsible for the poor learning, when in fact your initial definition of mastery might have been unrealistic or your initial mastery learning strategy might have been ineffective.

So, our second impulse is to say the following. If you belive that most of your students' failures to achieve mastery lay in how mastery was defined, then you might redefine mastery more appropriately and then regrade your students according to your new definition. Similarly if you believe that most of your students failed to achieve mastery because of how you taught, then you might want to adjust your students' grades accordingly.

We suggest that you continue to adjust your students' grades until such time that you believe you have a reasonable definition of mastery and an effective program for teaching for mastery. From then on, adhere closely to the mastery grading standard you have set.

Q. *Aren't you calling for a change in most schools grading practices?*

A. Yes. We do not want to throw out grades, but we do want a student's grade to accurately reflect what he has and has not learned rather than just how well he has learned relative to his peers. We feel that as long as students must constantly judge themselves against the learning of their peers they can never develop their own personal performance standards nor can they experience the pure pleasure of meeting such standards. The students would always need to refer to standards based on the performance of others so as to gauge his own performance.

On Reporting Grades

Q. *You have suggested how I might indicate to my students what their grades represent. How might I do the same for the students' parents?*

A. We would recommend that you send home a "goal card" based on each student's modified course table of specifications. To construct this goal card, simply list each objective in the student's table. Beside each objective then indicate whether the student mastered or did not master it. Table 5-1 is an example goal card taken from the Winnetka, Illinois, Public Schools (Airasian and Madaus, 1974).

On Evaluating Program Effectiveness

Q. *Isn't demanding that twice as many of my students earn "A"s when taught by mastery methods, as compared to non-mastery methods, a stringent criterion for evaluating my mastery program's effectiveness.*

Table 5-1. Portion of the Mathematics Goal Record Card of the
Winnetka Public Schools*

Recognizes number groups up to 5
Recognizes patterns of objects to 10   _____
Can count objects to 100   _____
Recognizes numbers to 100   _____
Can read and write numerals to 50   _____
Recognizes addition and subtraction symbols   _____
Understands meaning of the equality sign   _____
Understand meaning of the inequality signs   _____
Can count objects:
  by 2's to 20   _____
  by 5's to 100   _____
  by 10's to 100   _____
Recognizes geometric figures:
  triangle
  circle   _____
  quadrilateral   _____
Recognizes coins (1¢, 5¢, 10¢, 25¢)   _____
Knows addition combinations 10 and under using objects _____
Knows subtraction combinations 10 and under using objects _____
Recognizes addition and subtraction vertically and horizontally _____
Shows understanding of numbers and number combinations
  1. Using concrete objects
  2. Beginning to visualize and abstract   _____
  3. Makes automatic responses without concrete objects _____
    Can tell time   _____
  1. Hour
  2. Half hour   _____
  3. Quarter hour   _____
Addition combinations 10 and under (automatic response) _____
Subtraction combinations 10 and under (automatic response) _____
Can count to 200   _____
Can understand zero as a number   _____
Can understand place value to tens   _____
Can read and write numerals to 200   _____
Can read and write number words to 20   _____
Use facts in 2-digit column addition (no carrying)   _____
Roman numerals to XII   _____

*From P. W. Airasian and G. F. Madaus, "Criterion-Referenced Testing in the Class-room," in *Crucial Issues in Testing.* Edited by Ralph W. Tyler and Richard M. Wolf. Berkeley, Calif.: McCutchan Publishing Company, 1974, p. 80.

A. Yes. You may want to use a less stringent criterion. Some teachers, for example, have judged their mastery program to be effective when it has helped but one more student to earn an "A" grade then would typically be the case. Others have judged their program to be effective when it has helped 1.5 times as many students earn "A"s as would typically be the case.

Q. *Can I use the percentage of students who earned "B", "C", "D", and "F" grades as well as the percentage who earned "A"s to evaluate the overall effectiveness of my mastery learning program?*

A. Yes.

Q. *What are some of the basic reasons you have found for an ineffective mastery strategy?*

A. One reason is that the teacher did not really believe that all of his students could learn for mastery. A second is that the teacher failed to seriously undertake the planning that is required to teach for mastery. The teacher thought he could walk into class on the first day of the course and be teaching for mastery on day two. A third reason is that the teacher failed to orient his students to his mastery learning strategy— i.e., to what they were supposed to learn for mastery and/or how they were supposed to learn it. The fourth reason is that the teacher failed to execute his strategy. That is, the teacher failed to teach so that all students would learn. Perhaps the most common failure to execute we have found is that the teacher fails to implement the feedback/correction procedures he has developed. The final reason is that the teacher fails to revise his strategy using the casual and systematic information he has gathered about the strategy's effectiveness.

The *casual* information might consist of personal feelings, concerns, and impressions about the program; off-the-cuff feedback received from colleagues and students; and any notes, comments, etc., made on or in connection with the classroom instruction—e.g., comments in the textbook's margin, notes in a classroom diary, remarks in a daily lesson plan book, or any other data the teacher might have unintentionally gathered. The *systematic* information would consist of final examination results; unit diagnostic-progress test and retest results; the course and unit tables of specifications; each student's modified course table of specifications; data on corrective usage; and any other data might have intentionally gathered (e.g., questionnaire data, solicited opinions from colleagues).

References

Airasian, P. W. and Madaus, G. F.: "Criterion-Referenced Testing in the Classroom," in *Crucial Issues in Testing*. Edited by Ralph W. Tyler and

Richard M. Wolf. Berkeley, California: McCutchen Publishing Company, 1974, 73–87.

Block, J. H.: "Toward the Setting of Mastery Performance Standards in Veterinary Medicine," in *Learning Experiences,* Proceedings of the 5th Annual Symposium on Veterinary Medical Education. Edited by J. R. Welser, Athens, Georgia: U.S. Public Health Service, 1972.

Block, J. H.: "A Description and Comparison of Bloom's Learning for Mastery Strategy and Keller's Personalized System Instruction," in *School Society and Mastery Learning.* Edited by J. H. Block. New York: Holt, Rinehart and Winston, 1974, 16–26.

Bloom, B. S., "Mastery Learning and Its Implications for Curriculum Development," in *Confronting Curriculum Reform.* Edited by Elliot W. Eisner, New York: Little, Brown and Company, Inc., 1971, 17–49.

Bloom, B. S., Hastings, J. T. and Madaus, G. F.: *Handbook on Formative and Summative Evaluation of Student Learning.* New York: McGraw-Hill, 1971.

Coffman, W. E.: "Essay Examinations," in *Educational Measurement,* Second Edition. Edited by R. L. Thorndike. Washington, D.C.: American Council on Education, 1971, 271–302.

Guilford, J. P.: *Personality.* New York: McGraw-Hill, 1959.

Harrow, A. J.: *A Taxonomy of the Psychomotor Domain.* New York: David McKay, 1972.

Krathwohl, D. R., Bloom, B. S., and Masia, B. B.: *Taxonomy of Educational Objectives.* Handbook II: The Affective Domain. New York: David McKay, 1964.

Menges, R. J. and McGaghie, W. C. "Learning in Group Settings: Toward a Classification of Outcomes," *Educational Technology, 14* (1974), 56–60.

Sarason, S. B.: The Culture of the School and the Problem of Change. Boston: Allyn & Bacon, 1971.

Spady, W. G.: "The Sociological Implications of Mastery Learning," in *Schools, Society and Mastery Learning.* Edited by J. H. Block. New York: Holt, Rinehart and Winston, 1974, 91–116.

White, R. W.: "Motivation Reconsidered: The Concept of Competence," *Psychological Review, 66* (1959), 297–333.

Index

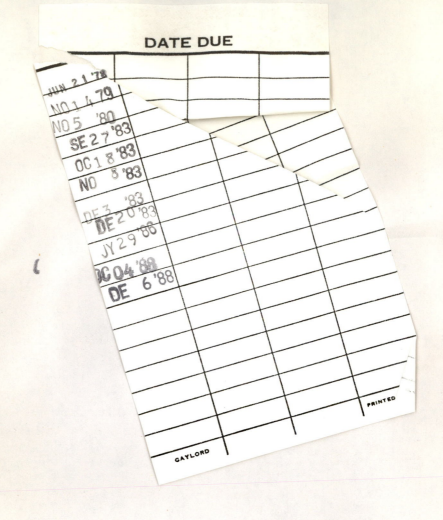